International Best Practice

Problem Management
A Practical Guide

London: TSO

tso
part of Williams Lea Tag

Published by TSO (The Stationery Office), part of Williams Lea, and available from:

Online
www.internationalbestpractice.com
www.tsoshop.co.uk

Mail, Telephone, Fax & E-mail
TSO
PO Box 29, Norwich, NR3 1GN
Telephone orders/General enquiries: 0333 202 5070
Fax orders: 0333 202 5080
E-mail: customer.services@tso.co.uk
Textphone 0333 202 5077

TSO@Blackwell and other Accredited Agents

International Best Practice (IBP) is a framework-neutral, independent imprint of TSO. We source, create and publish guidance which improves business processes and efficiency. We deliver an ever-expanding range of best-practice guidance and frameworks to a global audience.

© Propoint Solutions, Inc. 2016

All rights reserved. No part of this publication may be reproduced, stored in a retrieval system, or transmitted in any form or by any means, electronic, mechanical, photocopying, recording or otherwise without the permission of Propoint Solutions, Inc.

Applications for reproduction should be made in writing to Propoint Solutions, Inc., 9910 Palisade Ridge Drive, Colorado Springs, CO 80920, USA.

Copyright in the typographical arrangement, design and layout vests in the publisher, The Stationery Office Limited.

The information contained in this publication is believed to be correct at the time of manufacture. Whilst care has been taken to ensure that the information is accurate, the publisher can accept no responsibility for any errors or omissions or for changes to the details given.

A CIP catalogue record for this book is available from the British Library

A Library of Congress CIP catalogue record has been applied for

First published 2016
ISBN 9780117082984

Printed in the United Kingdom for The Stationery Office
P002794518   c3   09/16

Contents

List of figures ... v
List of tables ... vi
About this guide ... viii
Foreword ... xi
Preface ... xiii
Acknowledgements ... xiv

1 Problem management – an ITSM process ... 1
1.1 What is IT service management? ... 1
1.2 Processes and functions ... 5
1.3 ITSM terms and definitions ... 9
1.4 What is problem management? ... 11

2 Incident and problem management fundamentals ... 15
2.1 Introduction to the service resolution and restoration processes ... 15
2.2 Why incident management must be effective ... 17
2.3 The differences between incident and problem management ... 17
2.4 Common goals and objectives ... 19
2.5 A summary of similarities and differences between incident and problem management ... 19
2.6 Common process activities between incident and problem management ... 20

3 Problem management activities ... 35
3.1 Detection and categorization ... 40
3.2 Investigation and diagnosis (root cause analysis) ... 44
3.3 Resolution and recovery ... 66
3.4 Closure ... 70
3.5 Major problem review ... 74

4 Problem management relationships ... 77
4.1 Problem management's relationships to other ITSM processes ... 77
4.2 Problem management's relationship to ITSM functions ... 86

5 Organizing for problem management ... 91
5.1 Roles and responsibilities ... 92
5.2 RACI matrix ... 98
5.3 Organizational models ... 101
5.4 Tips on allocating resources ... 106

6		**Measuring problem management**	**109**
6.1		Why measure?	109
6.2		CSFs and KPIs	110
6.3		Management reporting	113
6.4		Process maturity assessments	115
7		**Keys to success**	**123**
7.1		Common success factors	123
7.2		Selling problem management – developing your business case	130
7.3		Addressing organizational change	135
7.4		Final thoughts	137

Appendices

A	Problem management policy template	139
B	Sample problem management plan table of contents	145
C	Problem management standard operating procedures template	147
D	Examples of symptom, resolution and root cause codes	169
E	Two-tier categorization scheme example	173
F	Service disruption report example	175
G	Sample project plan for process implementation	177
H	Communication plan template	189

Index 191

List of figures

Figure 1.1	Using best-practice standards and frameworks for delivering IT services	3
Figure 1.2	Services are delivered through a mix of people, process and technology	4
Figure 1.3	IT services supporting business processes	5
Figure 1.4	The main components that make up a process	7
Figure 1.5	Processes cross organizational boundaries	9
Figure 1.6	High-level overview of the problem management process	12
Figure 1.7	The two main aspects of problem management	13
Figure 2.1	Process flow for restoring and fixing errors in the infrastructure	16
Figure 2.2	Incident management process flow	21
Figure 2.3	Trending 'detected by' over time	23
Figure 2.4	Trending 'reported by' over time	24
Figure 2.5	Example of a multilevel categorization scheme	25
Figure 2.6	Incident matching and workarounds	33
Figure 3.1	Relationship between an incident, problem and root cause	36
Figure 3.2	Major categories and activities of problem management	36
Figure 3.3	Problem management process flow	39
Figure 3.4	Example of an Ishikawa diagram	57
Figure 3.5	Pareto chart of causes for customer dissatisfaction	59
Figure 3.6	Fault tree analysis diagram	65
Figure 3.7	Process record relationships	71
Figure 4.1	Relationships between ITSM processes, users and the service desk function	83
Figure 4.2	Problem management process relationships	85
Figure 5.1	Organizing for problem management in smaller IT organizations	102
Figure 5.2	Organizing for problem management in larger IT organizations	103
Figure 5.3	Centralized problem management organization	105
Figure 5.4	The task force organizational model	106
Figure 7.1	Adopter categorization	136
Figure 7.2	Reactions to organizational change	137
Figure C.1	Problem management high-level process flow	149
Figure C.2	Problem management process relationships	150
Figure C.3	Standard workflow symbols and abbreviations used within the workflow	152
Figure C.4	Identification and recording	154
Figure C.5	Categorization and resource allocation	157
Figure C.6	Investigate and diagnose: Part 1	159
Figure C.7	Investigate and diagnose: Part 2	161
Figure C.8	Solution identification	163
Figure C.9	Solution implementation	165
Figure C.10	Problem and known error closure	167

List of tables

Table 1.1	Generic process roles and responsibilities	8
Table 2.1	Similarities and differences between incident and problem management	19
Table 2.2	Common data to capture when logging	22
Table 2.3	Initial categorization of an incident	25
Table 2.4	Final categorization of an incident	26
Table 2.5	Example of an 'impact' level table	27
Table 2.6	Example of an 'urgency' level table	28
Table 2.7	Example of a prioritization model	28
Table 2.8	Expected level of effort based on priority	31
Table 2.9	Escalation scheme based on incident priority	32
Table 3.1	Common states of a problem record	38
Table 3.2	Reactive and proactive triggers for opening a problem record	40
Table 3.3	The six steps involved in investigation and diagnosis	45
Table 3.4	Questions to ask when defining a problem	46
Table 3.5	Example output from a brainstorming RCA technique	53
Table 3.6	Example of sorted events surrounding the scenario problem	55
Table 3.7	Pareto analysis of customer dissatisfaction with service desk	59
Table 3.8	'Could be' but 'is not' table	62
Table 3.9	'True if' table	63
Table 3.10	Setting time parameters for problems	69
Table 4.1	Service level management: inputs to and outputs from problem management	77
Table 4.2	Incident management: inputs to and outputs from problem management	78
Table 4.3	Change management: inputs to and outputs from problem management	79
Table 4.4	Release management: inputs to and outputs from problem management	79
Table 4.5	Configuration management: inputs to and outputs from problem management	80
Table 4.6	Knowledge management: inputs to and outputs from problem management	81
Table 4.7	Financial management: inputs to and outputs from problem management	81
Table 4.8	Capacity management: inputs to and outputs from problem management	82
Table 4.9	Supplier management: inputs to and outputs from problem management	83
Table 4.10	Examples of functional teams	87
Table 4.11	Inputs to and outputs from problem management by functional category	88
Table 5.1	Complementary roles supporting problem management	97
Table 5.2	Simplified RACI matrix for problem management	100
Table 6.1	Common CSFs and KPIs for problem management	111
Table 6.2	Additional KPIs to consider for problem management	113
Table 6.3	Example of common problem management reports	116
Table 7.1	Process training mapped to process roles	129
Table D.1	Sample symptom codes for incidents and problems	169

Table D.2	Sample resolution codes for incidents and problems	170
Table D.3	Sample root cause codes for incidents and problems	171
Table E.1	Sample two-tier incident and problem categorization scheme	173
Table G.1	Project plan for designing and implementing a process	178
Table H.1	Communication plan	190

About this guide

Who's it for?

One of the challenges in writing this guide was determining the target audience of readers. The smallest IT organization that we have worked with to successfully implement problem management had an entire staff of six people, including the CIO. We recall asking the CIO how they could expect to perform problem management with an IT staff of six. Their response was sincere, and should inspire us all: 'On Friday afternoons, if there are no major issues, we will stop doing reactive incident management and focus for the next four hours as a team to identify the root cause and resolve our top problem for the week.' If an IT organization of six can do problem management, then this title is for everyone. Small organizations will find guidance on initiating their problem management process, while large organizations will discover numerous ideas that may be quickly applied to elevate their problem management process maturity to levels 3 to 4 and higher on the Capability Maturity Model Integration (CMMI) process maturity scale.

This title is intended for those who wish to gain a working knowledge of industry best practices related to problem management. It is ideal for IT professionals who are working, or plan to work, within problem management, whether in a technical, managerial or operational role.

Why do you need it?

This publication serves as the definitive resource for individuals and organizations looking to establish and mature the problem management process within their organization. It consolidates concepts and principles found across numerous IT service management (ITSM) frameworks, then adds the collective experiences of industry experts into an easy-to-read, practical and insightful guide. The bonus materials in the appendices provide templates, workflows and tools that can be leveraged by the reader to accelerate the maturity of their problem management process.

Problem Management: A Practical Guide is fully aligned with and serves as an expanded resource for the Problem Management Professional certification course offered by HDI®.

Who's it by?

Jim Bolton

Jim has more than a decade of experience in designing and delivering ITSM solutions. He is the founder and president of Propoint Solutions, Inc. (www.propointsolutions.com), an ITIL® training and ITSM process consulting organization. Jim is an expert at diagnosing and solving complex organizational and process challenges. Jim is an ITSM consultant, courseware developer, trainer, author and speaker at conferences around the world on ITSM topics. He received the IT Industry Legend award in 2014.

Jim's credentials include an MBA in technology management, ITIL v2 Manager, ITIL v3 Expert, ITIL Practitioner and Competency certificates and the *it*SMF ISO/IEC 20000 Consultant certificate.

Buff Scott III

Buff has more than 35 years of information technology experience, ranging from a technical programmer to an IT assistant vice-president of a large Fortune 500 company. He is a seasoned IT professional whose experience includes leading technical, operational, compliance, and process design and implementation teams. He has presented at numerous local and national ITSM conferences and forums and was the master of ceremonies at the 2006 *it*SMF-USA national conference.

Buff holds a BA in business administration and the ITIL v2 Manager, the ITIL v3 Expert and Certified Information Systems Auditor (CISA) certifications. He is an EXIN-accredited ITIL trainer, TIPA lead assessor for ITIL and the lead subject matter expert and instructor on the HDI Problem Management Professional certification course.

How is it organized?

As the title suggests, this is a practical guide to IT problem management, with an emphasis on providing ITSM and industry best practices and guidance. Examples, figures and tables, including personal examples based on Jim Bolton's experiences, are used throughout to illustrate the most important points, concepts and principles.

Designed to be read from start to finish, the text is organized into seven chapters, with the first two chapters setting the context for problem management as an ITSM process, and explaining problem management's interdependent relationship with incident management. Once the big picture has been explained, the subsequent chapters delve deeper into problem management activities; its relationship to other ITSM processes; and how to organize for, and measure, your problem management process.

The publication ends with several appendices that provide real-life examples of process artefacts that can be used in the design and implementation of a problem management process. A summary of what is covered in each chapter is as follows:

- **Chapter 1** Provides an introduction to IT service management and problem management as an ITSM process, and defines terms and definitions that will be used throughout the remainder of the text.

- **Chapter 2** Shows the relationship and interdependency between incident and problem management as service resolution and restoration processes. Their similarities and differences are explained as well as their common goals, objectives and activities.

- **Chapter 3** Explains in detail the major activities and tasks associated with problem management. It considers how problem management activities are performed and explores seven common industry root cause analysis techniques.

- **Chapter 4** Examines the relationship of problem management to other ITSM processes and functions, including their inputs to, and outputs from, problem management. Processes included are: service level management; incident management; change management; configuration management; release management; knowledge management; financial management; capacity management; and supplier/vendor management. The functions include infrastructure functions, customer-facing functions and operations functions.

- **Chapter 5** Describes the different primary and complementary roles and responsibilities associated with problem management, and provides examples of various organizational models that can be implemented for the performance of problem management activities.

- **Chapter 6** Presents the common critical success factors, key performance indicators, and metrics used to measure the effectiveness and efficiency of a mature problem management process.

- **Chapter 7** Provides a list and explanation of the common success factors for implementing problem management; how to avoid common pitfalls; and how to 'sell' the value of problem management to your organization.

Foreword

David Cannon, vice-president and consulting director, Forrester Research

Problem management exists in most organizations, yet often does not achieve its full potential – frequently being relegated to a call-out box in the incident management process: 'resolve root cause'.

Problem Management: A Practical Guide embraces and expounds on the progress made over the last two decades while addressing the challenges that many organizations have experienced in attempting to achieve everything that problem management promised. It addresses three important areas that have limited problem management's success:

- **Technologists** While technologists frequently know how to diagnose root causes, interpret trends and keep equipment running, they often restrict the scope of problem management to their technical expertise. This disconnects the activities of keeping systems running from the activities of delivering true business value.
- **Tool vendors** Many tool vendors find the complexity of problem management difficult to deal with and focus on basic reactive techniques, such as detecting repeat incidents. While tool functionality has expanded, most implementations do not go beyond these basic tasks.
- **Best practices** Practitioners sometimes treat guidelines as absolute rules, and spend more time arguing over 'what the book says' than what problem management needs to achieve.

Throughout this guide, the authors challenge practitioners to take a more practical approach to problem management, specifically addressing:

- The notion that 'incident management' equals 'service desk' and that 'problem management' equals 'technical support'. Any approach that confuses a process with an organizational unit will run into turbulent political waters.
- Approaches that view problem management as a component of incident management. Every practitioner agrees that incidents and problems are related (and sometimes coincide) but that they are also different. Yet some practitioners fuse the processes and dilute the effectiveness of both.
- The practice of separating problem management from technical groups that use the process most. This guide views problem management as essential to enhance existing technology management activities.

Most importantly, *Problem Management: A Practical Guide* shows problem management to be a core business competency that is critical for the reliability and availability of the technology that makes an organization successful.

Rick Joslin, former executive director, HDI

The problem management process should be a core process in every organization's service management strategy. Yet many organizations have not implemented it formally and others struggle with it, often because of the lack of industry guidance and the lack of best-practice understanding. Throughout this guide, Jim and Buff have continued their personal missions to help organizations be more successful by sharing their expertise with the industry.

Historically, support organizations have focused heavily on optimizing incident management. The support analysts are the first responders and in the frontline when their customers are in need of assistance. Like fire-fighters, support analysts respond to resolve incidents in order to quickly restore services. If that is all the support organizations did, they would always be in a reactive state of fire-fighting incidents. By implementing problem management support, organizations are proactively investigating high-impact incidents and frequently recurring incidents. Problem management professionals have a role similar to those of the fire marshal and fire investigators. They must investigate and identify the root cause of the problems that generate incidents, with the ultimate purpose of eliminating the causes and/or identifying more effective resolutions when an incident occurs.

Technical support professionals and problem management professionals must work as one team, capturing and sharing knowledge to improve the quality of products and services while improving the bottom line for stakeholders. Knowledge management is a key connector between incident and problem management. When knowledge is captured, improved and reused within incident management by support professionals, valuable metadata is created to aid problem managers. As problem managers learn through their investigations, they share that knowledge with the support professionals by updating the knowledge base. Thus, support organizations need to master incident, knowledge and problem management to better service their customers.

The ultimate goal of a problem manager is not to manage problems, but to determine how to eliminate them. *Problem Management: A Practical Guide* will help professionals improve their personal knowledge and skills to investigate the problems that exist within their organizations. Organizations no longer need to struggle and experiment with problem management, as they can now learn from the experts.

Preface

One of the characteristics that high-performing IT organizations have in common is that they have a formal and well-defined problem management process. They recognize the need to move beyond the futility of merely resolving recurring incidents, and are determined to invest resources in identifying, documenting, investigating and permanently removing underlying problems from their computing environment.

While incident management focuses on restoring service as quickly as possible, problem management focuses on determining the root cause, identifying temporary workarounds and applying permanent fixes so that incidents do not reoccur. By analysing real-time and historical data, problem management can identify potential failures and correct issues before the customer is affected. Imagine meeting with your customers to tell them about 'the incident that never happened'!

The content of this publication is not intended to provide detailed instruction on root cause analysis (RCA) techniques. There have been several good books written on this topic, and there are organizations in the industry that provide in-depth training on these techniques. We will, however, introduce seven common RCA techniques and provide examples of their application.

Several years ago Propoint Solutions developed a problem management course based on feedback from our customers who were asking for guidance on how to improve their IT services. Since then, problem management has been the most popular process course that we have offered. In 2013 we partnered with HDI to establish standards and develop an expanded problem management professional certification course. The first such course was delivered in 2014, and since that time we have continued to expand and mature a body of knowledge around problem management from the experiences shared by colleagues and students in the classes. Many of those students have asked if we would write a book to provide them with additional guidance, templates and tools to help them develop and mature their problem management process. It is our hope that this publication will serve the needs of those students, and many others in our industry who are looking for guidance to improve their problem management process.

Jim Bolton
Buff Scott III

Acknowledgements

We would particularly like to thank Dr Erik Jagel for contributing his expert knowledge and deep industry experience in both the content and the editing of this publication. We are also grateful to our many industry colleagues for their generous support and encouragement in writing this title. A special word of thanks goes out to our wives, Debbie and Sandy, who have unfailingly supported and encouraged us throughout this new 'chapter' in our careers.

About the reviewers

Maysam Abedian

Maysam is the change, service introduction and major incident manager at Williams Lea Tag (Deutsche Post DHL group) and is an ITIL qualified professional with more than 15 years of industry experience, from both a technical and an ITSM background. He has been involved in implementing ITSM and service transition processes, as well as service desk functions and ITSM toolsets within organizations. Maysam's background includes a BSc degree in mathematics and computing and an MSc degree in information systems management.

Andy Atencio

Andy is the chief technology officer for the City of Greenwood Village, Colorado, USA, where he and his team have implemented many of the ITIL best practices. He has been involved with ITSM for more than 15 years, and is ITIL Expert certified. Andy has been using his experience in psychological assessment tools and a master's degree in psychology to educate other technology leaders and organizations that true technology leadership begins with people.

John Custy

John is the managing consultant at JPC Group and has spent his career working in IT and service management organizations, providing a practical and pragmatic approach to service management by putting people and outcomes first, then the processes, and finally the technology. He has helped organizations to improve the value of their services by showing service providers how their services impact outcomes. He has worked with all types of organizations and business units, including financial services, healthcare, pharmaceutical, higher education, manufacturing, non-profit and government agencies. He is also a well-known educator and speaker on service management.

1 Problem management – an ITSM process

> **Learning from others – Jim's experience**
>
> Many years ago I was hired by a technology start-up to bring my manufacturing process background and quality engineering experiences to the IT industry. At the time, it seemed odd to me because the industries were so different. Manufacturing was focused on identifying bottlenecks, and developing processes to make sure every activity was repeatable and predictable. IT saw processes as 'boring and non-creative'.
>
> As I had the opportunity to assess numerous IT organizations throughout this new career, I discovered that successful IT organizations often followed a very similar and effective set of processes, while unsuccessful IT organizations often expressed that processes were constraining and slowed things down. As I continued to observe successful IT organizations, I documented their processes and integrated those processes into our growing company.
>
> At one point, a friend heard what I was doing and suggested I might be interested in taking an ITSM class to learn more about best-practice processes for an IT organization. Initially I disregarded the idea as I already had processes that were working for us. Months later, I purchased a set of books on ITSM best practices and began reading. Honestly, I was looking for mistakes in the books to prove my friend wrong and to validate my belief that no one had better IT processes than ours.
>
> Initially I was surprised to find that the processes described in the books were very similar to the processes we were using. However, I did find some 'mistakes' in the books, which I happily highlighted with red adhesive tabs so I could later show them to my friend. Over the next months I tried some of the new ideas I found in the books and discovered they addressed issues that we were having with our current processes. I still have those books with the red tabs in my library as a reminder that we can all learn from the experiences of others.

Before jumping right into problem management, let's begin by introducing/reviewing some fundamental ITSM concepts and terms.

1.1 What is IT service management?

'Service' is work performed on behalf of another that delivers value to the customer by enabling the customer to achieve desired organizational outcomes. IT service management (ITSM) is a methodology for planning, developing, delivering and managing IT services that are customer-focused and process-driven. It is about delivering services that are reliable and available. It is the effective and efficient application and management of service assets by the IT service provider for the purpose of delivering services that bring value to the customer by enabling them to achieve their desired outcomes.

IT service providers continue to face new challenges and opportunities that require them to adapt to an ever-changing business environment. Successful and innovative companies develop good practices, which evolve into best practices and eventually accepted practice, and in some cases they even become industry requirements. There are several ITSM best-practice frameworks available and it is common for IT service providers to make use of one or more of these. Some of the more widely known and used ITSM frameworks are:

- ITIL®
- MOF (Microsoft Operations Framework)
- ITUP 7 (IBM® Tivoli® Unified Process Operations Framework).

While it can be argued that ITIL is the most globally known and widely accepted ITSM framework in the world, there are a number of best practices, frameworks and standards that IT service providers commonly use when delivering services, such as:

- COBIT (Control OBjectives for Information and related Technology)
- SDLC (Software Development Lifecycle)
- ISO/IEC 20000 (an international standard for ITSM)
- PRINCE2® (PRojects IN Controlled Environments)
- Six Sigma (elimination of defects)
- TQM (Total Quality Management)
- Deming Cycle
- Agile
- DevOps
- PMI® (Project Management Institute)
- CMMI (Capability Maturity Model Integration)
- KCS (Knowledge Centered Support).

As IT organizations successfully adopt and adapt best practices, they will mature in the way they deliver services. Successfully using these best-practice frameworks and the 'Plan–Do–Check–Act' (PDCA) cycle made popular by William Deming,[1] they are able to reach higher levels of maturity. Over time, organizations will move from a fire-fighting and reactive mode, to becoming more proactive and delivering services of value to the business that are aligned with business plans and objectives. Additionally, as best-practice frameworks are in place, they keep organizations from sliding backwards over time. Figure 1.1 shows the maturity progression of an IT service provider as they use best-practice ITSM standards and frameworks.

Using these best practices, standards and frameworks provides benefits for the IT service provider and the businesses they support. Those benefits include:

- Increased productivity
- Increased customer satisfaction

---

[1] Dr William Deming is credited with transforming the automotive manufacturing processes in Japan after World War II by using the continual service improvement model, often referred to as the 'Plan–Do–Check–-Act' cycle developed by Dr Walter Shewhart.

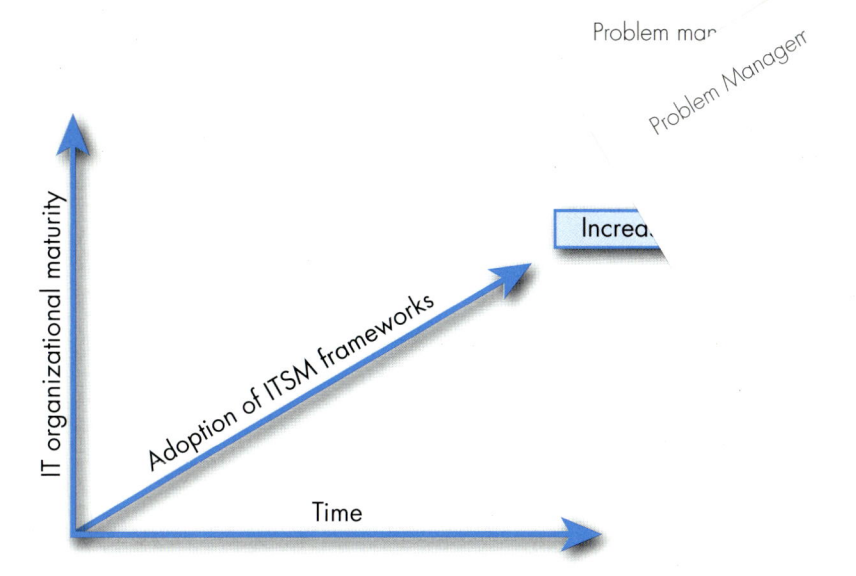

Figure 1.1 Using best-practice standards and frameworks for delivering IT services

- Reduced risk
- Reduced costs
- Improved communications and alignment between IT and the customer
- Consistent and predictable levels of IT support
- Customers know what to expect and what is expected of them
- Improved efficiency and effectiveness in delivering IT services
- IT services become part of the business strategy.

In Figure 1.2, we see a sample of services that an IT service provider might make available to its customers (e.g. email, web hosting, print services). The services should be delivered efficiently, effectively and predictably through the use of common and standardized processes.

Note
The customer may be internal (within the same organization) or external to the organization. Likewise, the IT service provider may be internal or external to the organization.

It's the outcome that's important – Jim's experience
As a customer, I take my shirts to a dry cleaning and laundry business. I don't know what kind of washing machine, or iron, or laundry detergent they are using, and I don't really care as long as my shirts are clean and pressed and delivered on time. It's the outcome, laundered shirts, which I am interested in.

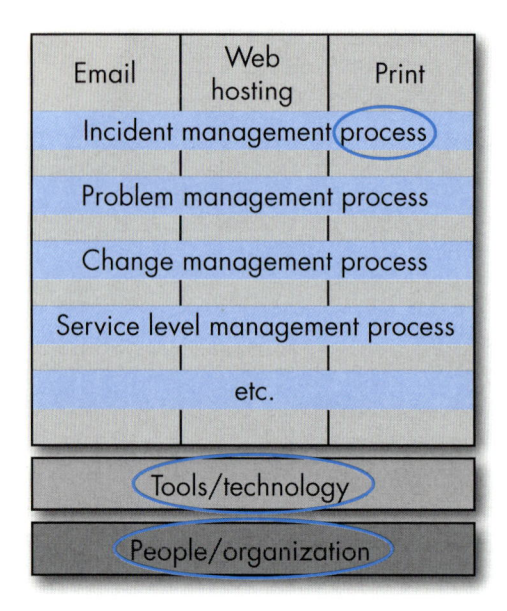

Figure 1.2 Services are delivered through a mix of people, process and technology

When we talk about IT services we're not simply talking about technology, we're talking about those services that directly support the business processes. In Figure 1.3 we see a number of different business units, each with their own business processes. We also see that the business processes are supported by IT services and those services are underpinned and supported by infrastructure. While it is necessary and important to manage servers, those servers are merely a means to the end. Delivery of a service that provides value to the customer is the goal.

If we identify IT service 1 as email, we can see that there are a number of technology components required to deliver the email service to the user. The user or customer is not interested in the technology components; they are simply interested in having email at their desk and knowing that when they hit the 'send/receive' button, their email will be successfully delivered and received.

> **Note**
> It is important to have your IT services well defined and documented, preferably in a service catalogue, for use by both IT staff and the business. If your services are not currently defined, begin with a list of strategic business customers or units and meet with key stakeholders in those areas to identify and define their vital business functions. A vital business function is a mission-critical function that the business depends upon and without which they cannot continue, where the financial or operational impact of the function becoming lost or degraded is not acceptable. Often, vital business function names reflect the actual service that IT is providing to the customer.

Problem management – an ITSM process

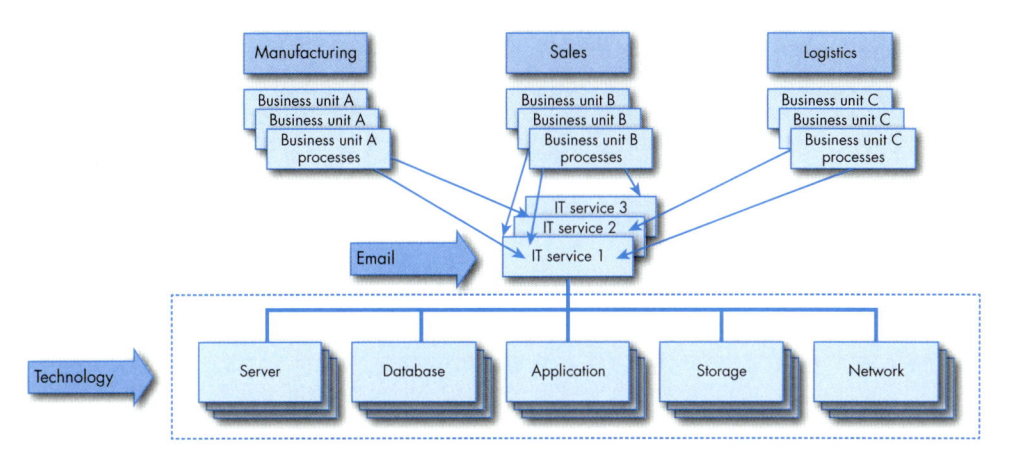

Figure 1.3 IT services supporting business processes

1.2 Processes and functions

> **We all need processes and functions – Jim's experience**
> Just as an IT organization needs processes and functions, so does my dry cleaners and laundry that I mentioned above. They have processes for receiving laundry, for washing, for drying, for ironing and for receiving payment. They also have people and/or equipment responsible for each of the specific functions within their organization.

Successful ITSM is dependent upon the use of well-defined, standardized and repeatable processes. In fact, one could say that ITSM is more process-focused and tied to process improvement efforts than it is about technology. Although not limited to just IT, these processes should span the various organizational departments or functional teams such as the applications team, the operations team and the network team. The reason we need processes to span these functional teams is because many of our daily IT organizational activities involve all of these teams working together. For instance, when email breaks and the user calls the service desk to report an outage, initially the service desk would not know whether the ticket should be assigned to the applications team, the operations team or the network team, because potentially the outage could need to be fixed by any of those teams. Thus, the incident management process spans all of those functional teams. With problem management the same is true. When we do a root cause analysis for email outages, we may need to pull together these same teams in order to get to the root cause. When scheduling a change to remove the error from the environment, the same is true again. We need to ensure that various functional teams approve the change and that the service desk has awareness of it so they can communicate any anticipated change-related impacts to the customer. From an ITSM perspective, processes span the functional teams and bring higher levels of efficiency and effectiveness.

In smaller organizations, the focus may not be on bringing together different teams, but rather about making sure the right individuals are involved. In a small organization the same person might be responsible for multiple functions, and in these instances the individual with responsibility for the service desk might also be required to assist in finding the root cause of a problem.

1.2.1 Processes

> **If manufacturers can do it, why can't IT? – Jim's experience**
> In manufacturing we had detailed processes for every activity on the production line. A new employee was able to pick up a process document (work instructions) and read how to successfully complete a specific manufacturing task. Any variation in manufacturing that was causing a product defect could be traced back to a poorly written process, lack of proper training, or an enforcement issue where an individual chose not to follow the process. Unfortunately, not all IT organizations are this disciplined. IT processes were often described as 'tribal knowledge'. I am frequently asked, 'Why do we need to write these things down when everyone knows the right thing to do'. Or, 'It's my job; I don't want someone telling me how to do my job.' Lastly, I sometimes hear about IT organizations that have documented their IT processes but failed to follow and/or enforce those processes. We refer to these procedures as 'write once read never'.

A process is a set of related activities that work together to provide value to the customer. They are designed to accomplish a specific objective by taking a set of inputs and transforming them into one or more outputs. Processes typically respond to a particular trigger or event. As an example, the incident management process may be triggered by a call to the service desk. The trigger for problem management will most often be one or more incidents.

A mature process is defined, documented, communicated/trained, measured and enforced. It should have an assigned owner, a set of activities, and procedures and work instructions that are performed by people and/or technology. It should be measured in terms of cost, quality, speed to delivery and compliance.

The three main components that make up a process are listed below and represented in Figure 1.4:

- Process controls
- Process structure
- Process enablers.

1.2.1.1 Process documentation

A well-documented process should have three process 'control' documents: the process policy, the plan and standard operating procedures (SOPs):

Problem management – an ITSM process

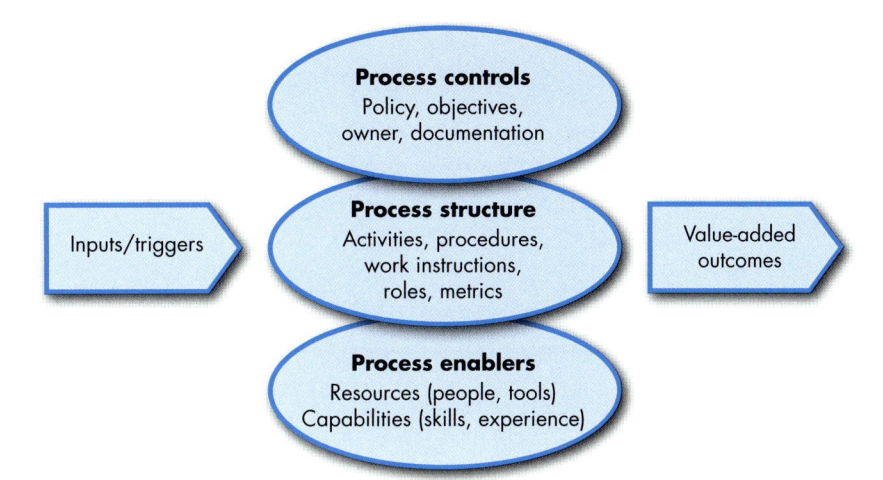

Figure 1.4 The main components that make up a process

- **Policy** Communicates management's intent and expectations regarding the process. (An example of a problem management policy is provided in Appendix A.)
- **Plan** Communicates the 'what' and the 'why' of the process, the goals and purpose, the roles and responsibilities, the metrics and the measurements to be used for the process, training requirements and tool access requirements. This plan needs to be specific to your organization (see the table of contents in Appendix B for help in structuring your problem management plan).
- **SOP** Communicates how to perform the process using the supporting tools. The SOP shows who's doing what tasks and in what order, and screenshots and detailed work instructions explain how those tasks and activities are performed using available tools that support the process (see Appendix C for an example of a problem management SOP).

These documents are necessary to ensure enterprise-wide understanding, and for the successful implementation and performance of the process. Documentation should be detailed, include activities, tasks and procedures, and must be complete, available and maintained to reflect the current process requirements.

1.2.1.2 Process roles

There are three common roles for every ITSM process. These roles are process owner, process manager and process analyst (also called 'process engineer' or 'process practitioner'). Table 1.1 provides a summary of the responsibilities of each of these generic roles. (We will discuss the specific roles related to problem management in Chapter 5.)

Table 1.1 Generic process roles and responsibilities

Role	Responsibilities
Process owner	Has overall accountability for a specific process, any design effort associated with that process, and ongoing process performance and improvement
	Ensures that the process and related policies are clearly defined, designed, documented, communicated, trained and performed to meet the needs of the customers/stakeholders
	Addresses process compliance issues
Process manager	Responsible for daily operational management of a process and for monitoring compliance with the process
	Works with the process owner to plan and coordinate all process activities and ensures all activities are carried out
	Monitors and reports on the performance of the process and identifies opportunities for improvement
Process analyst	Responsible for carrying out one or more process activities
	May be internal or external personnel (e.g. suppliers, contractors, service partners, or even customers/users)
	Works with other stakeholders (e.g. process manager, co-workers, customers) to ensure their actions are effective
	Ensures all their process activities, including inputs, outputs and interfaces to other processes, are properly executed
	Creates or updates problem records throughout their lifecycle to show that activities have been carried out correctly

1.2.2 Functions

> **Functions and processes – Jim's experience**
> When the service desk receives a phone call from a user complaining that their email is not working, this could be a network issue, a server issue, an application issue, a desktop issue, a mobile device issue, or possibly even operator error. IT organizations typically have functions (sometimes referred to as technical support groups) that are responsible for each of these technology domains. Each of these functions has their own body of knowledge and expertise. The processes we described earlier allow each of these functional teams to focus on their area of expertise while working together seamlessly with no overlaps and no gaps.

Functions, or functional teams, are units of organizations specialized to perform certain types of work and to be responsible for specific outcomes. They consist of a group of people and the service assets they use to carry out one or more process activities. These functional teams are often referred to as technical support groups within IT organizations and are typically defined by the technology domains they support.

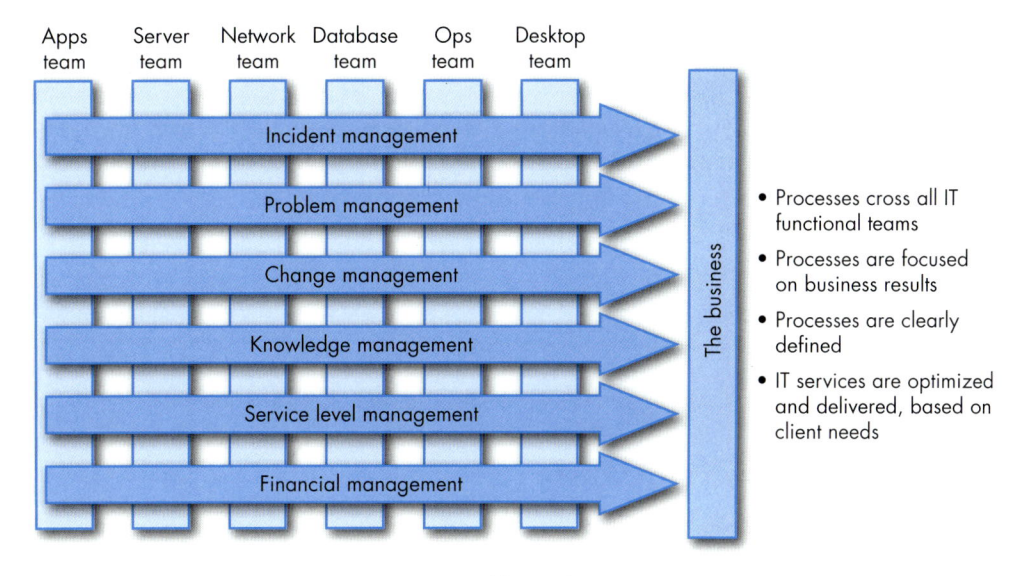

Figure 1.5 Processes cross organizational boundaries

- Processes cross all IT functional teams
- Processes are focused on business results
- Processes are clearly defined
- IT services are optimized and delivered, based on client needs

Functions:

- Have defined roles and the associated authority and responsibility for specific performance and outcomes
- Have their own body of knowledge (that accumulates from experience)
- Provide structure and stability to organizations
- Optimize their work methods locally to focus on assigned outcomes
- Have their own terminology/language.

Processes help to improve cross-functional coordination and to ensure that functional teams are focused on business outcomes. Poor coordination between functions, combined with an inward focus, can lead to functional silos that hinder alignment and feedback critical to the success of an organization as a whole. Well-defined processes will reduce 'finger pointing' and improve productivity within and across the functional teams. Figure 1.5 illustrates how processes span organizational boundaries.

1.3 ITSM terms and definitions

ITSM provides a common language to facilitate the sharing of ideas. This has become even more important as organizations consider outsourcing portions of their IT operations. As an example, imagine how confusing it can be when many different words are being used to describe a service that is not performing as expected. Historically, those terms have included error, failure, outage, ticket, break fix, incident, event, problem and issue.

Problem Management

Before we go any further, we need to introduce some other terms that will be used throughout the rest of this publication:

- **Configuration item** (CI) An IT component that is recorded, managed and reported on via the configuration management process and controlled via the change management process. Examples of CI categories typically include IT services, hardware, software, buildings, people, and formal documentation such as process documentation and service level agreements.

- **Configuration management database** (CMDB) The CMDB is a database used to store configuration records throughout their lifecycle. Each CMDB stores attributes of CIs and their relationships to other CIs. The CMDB is the foundation of the configuration management process and is used by a number of ITSM processes. The CMDB is part of the configuration management system.

- **Configuration management system** A system and set of tools used for storing various types of data and process records, including incident, problem, change, release and configuration management records.

- **Customer** A person who purchases goods and services and is authorized to negotiate service level agreements. A customer may also be a user.

- **Incident** An unplanned event that disrupts the normal operation of a service, or causes a reduction in the quality of that service. This can include the failure of an IT component that has not yet impacted a service. In essence, something is broken or not working as expected. Incidents may be one-time events, major events or repetitive in nature.

- **Knowledge base** A searchable database of structured information and data pertaining to specific topics.

- **Known error** A problem that has a documented root cause and workaround.

- **Known error database** A database (or in some organizations a knowledge base) used to store previous knowledge of incidents and problems (symptoms, workarounds and solutions) enabling quicker diagnosis and resolution in the future.

- **Problem** The cause or potential cause of incidents where the root cause is not usually known.

- **Root cause** The cause of an incident or problem to which a fix may be applied to resolve or prevent recurrence.

- **Solution** An identified means of resolving an incident or problem that permanently fixes the underlying root cause.

- **User** A person who uses IT services as part of their day-to-day work activities.

- **Workaround** A temporary method of reducing or eliminating the impact of an incident until a permanent resolution is available.

1.4 What is problem management?

> **Tip**
> Problem management is one of the core ITSM processes that an IT service provider should have in their service delivery toolkit. Providing a stable and available computing environment is not possible when the IT service provider does not possess the ability to effectively react to and prevent service disruptions.

Problem management is recognized as the ITSM process where trends and causal factors are analysed to determine the root cause of one or more incidents. This information is then used for the development of workarounds and resolutions to those incidents. As we will see in later chapters, problems have a lifecycle. The purpose of problem management is to manage all problems throughout their lifecycle from detection, to logging, to categorizing and prioritizing, investigation and diagnosis, documentation and eventual removal of the error from the computing environment. Problem management records and reports information that enables end-to-end visibility of problems. It provides accurate and reliable data on problem management activities to IT and the business. This information includes the status of problems and known errors, root causes and trend analysis, workarounds and resolutions, and compliance with the process.

The activities associated with problem management can be organized into four major categories:

- **Detection and categorization** Those activities focused on identifying, logging, classifying and prioritizing problems
- **Investigation and diagnosis** Those activities focused on identifying root causes and transforming problems into known errors
- **Resolution and recovery** Those activities focused on identifying, approving, applying and validating permanent fixes to problems and known errors
- **Closure** Those activities focused on closing problems, known errors and related incidents with updated and reusable information

Figure 1.6 reflects these four categories of major activities and provides a summary of the tasks associated with each.

1.4.1 Reactive versus proactive

The scope of problem management includes two different aspects – reactive problem management and proactive problem management.

Reactive problem management is focused on solving problems in response to one or more incidents as they occur. Proactive problem management is focused on identifying and solving

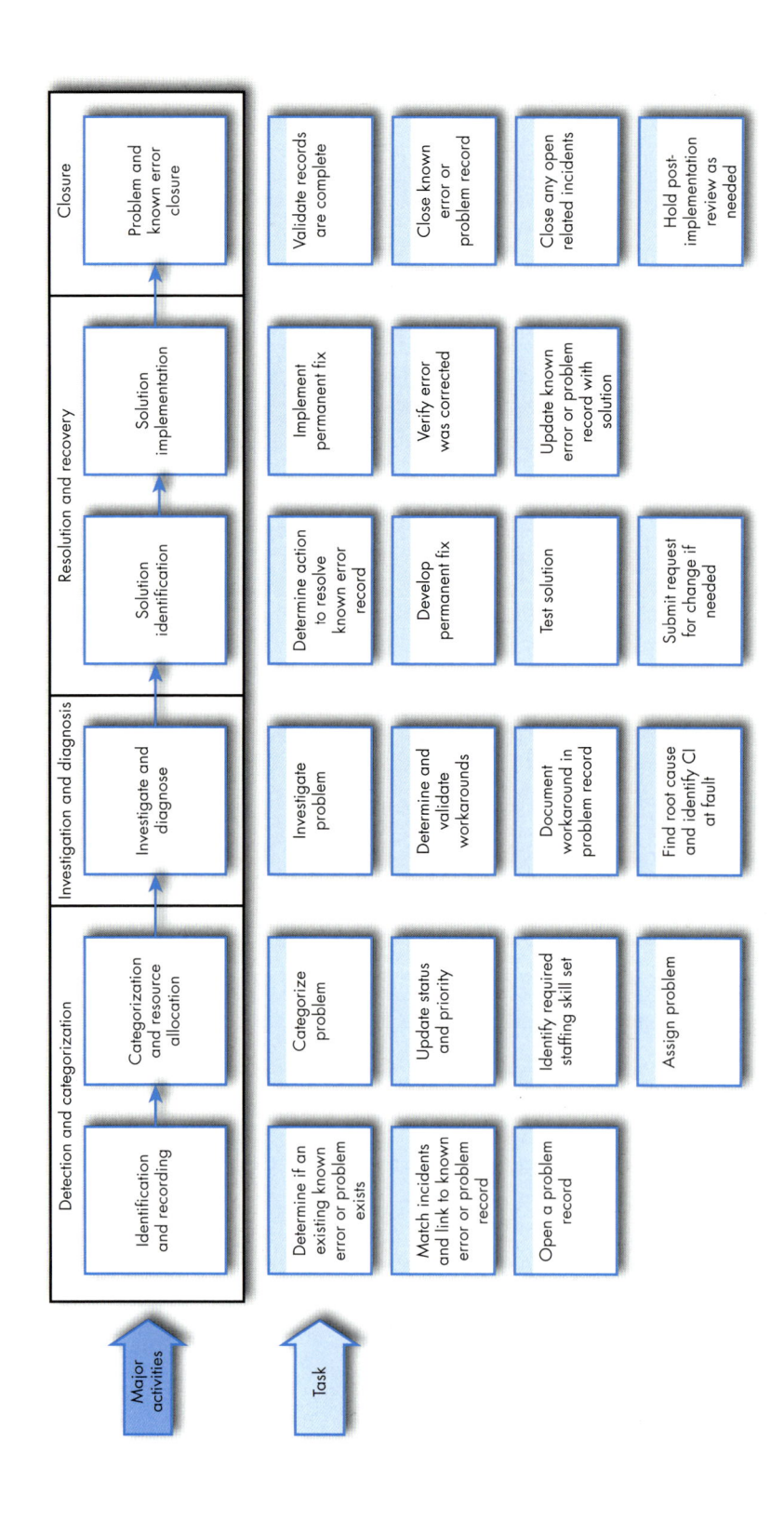

Figure 1.6 High-level overview of the problem management process

> **Is it worth being proactive? – Jim's experience**
> We frequently experience internet service outages in the neighbourhood. When I call our service provider to advise them of the outage they say they are sorry and hope to have it repaired soon. They always offer a service credit to my next bill reflecting the duration of the service outage. The credit amounts to around one pound when the internet is down for an entire day. It's my opinion that bad service for free is still bad service. In contrast, our local utility company sends out an advance notice to let us know that they will be performing preventive maintenance to replace a water line which is aging and nearing the end of its useful life. Our utility company even sends out a newsletter each month to let us know about proactive work they are doing in other parts of our city. I love our utility company for being proactive. It's possible that we pay a bit more because of their proactive work. However, I suspect that it's much less expensive to schedule the replacement of a water line than it would be to call out an emergency crew and equipment after a pipe bursts. Perhaps our internet service provider could learn a lesson from our utility company. Perhaps there is a lesson in this for all of us.

problems and known errors that might otherwise be missed (e.g. a database gradually running out of disk space), looking for trends and patterns, staying abreast of known errors from suppliers and community groups, and solving problems before incidents occur or reoccur. This analytical activity by problem management captures and reviews operational, maintenance and event logs to identify underlying problems and to understand the IT infrastructure's stability, usage and criticality in support of the business environment. By analysing that information, problem management is able to foresee and correct errors before the manifestation of incidents. In this sense, the process becomes proactive.

Proactive problem management is focused on:

- Identifying problems before they are experienced by the business
- Preventing problems from occurring (i.e. eliminating potential incidents and conflicts within the infrastructure)
- Reducing the probability that an identified risk will occur and/or implementing steps to reduce the impact should the problem occur
- Gathering lessons learned from major problem reviews for continuous improvement purposes
- Improving service quality and reliability.

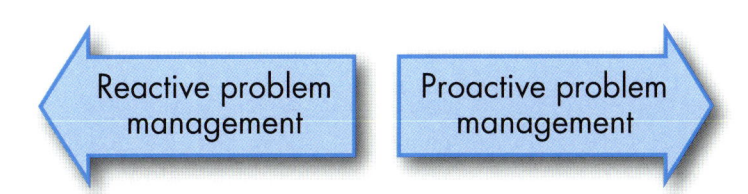

Figure 1.7 The two main aspects of problem management

Figure 1.7 reflects the two aspects of problem management. Notice the reactive arrow is pointing backwards (i.e. an incident has occurred) while the proactive arrow is pointing forward (i.e. looking ahead to identify potential incidents).

Problem management is more than just restoring services and applying permanent fixes to incidents, it is also about providing a stable and available infrastructure that supports business processes. Common benefits of implementing problem management are:

- Higher availability and reliability of IT services – i.e. improved service quality
- Higher productivity of the users and IT staff
- Increased customer satisfaction with IT
- Shorter resolution times (i.e. improved time to restore service) through collaboration and use of workarounds
- Improved management information reporting on problems and their status
- Reduction in costs for the management and resolution of incidents and problems
- Higher levels of compliance with service level agreements
- Reduction in time spent resolving problems by having a standardized approach – no more trial and error
- Reduction in incident volume (by eliminating recurring incidents)
- Improved first-call resolution through better information in the known error database or knowledge base
- Improved use and allocation of IT support staff
- Reduction in duplication of effort among functional teams in the development and application of workarounds and solutions to incidents
- Improved information, documentation, knowledge transfer and decision-making for support of the infrastructure
- More effective purchasing and asset management through a better understanding of problematic IT components
- Ability to identify under-engineered systems.

When performed well, problem management is an indication of a more mature IT service provider. However, research has shown that problem management is not performed at all, or is merely 'under development' in 51% of IT organizations surveyed.[2] Implementing problem management can be challenging; however, for those companies who have invested in implementing a best-practice problem management process, the payoff has been significant. So, how did they do it? What made them successful where others have failed?

---

2   Rains, Jenny (2014). Problem management in technical support. *HDI Research Brief,* April 2014.

2 Incident and problem management fundamentals

2.1 Introduction to the service resolution and restoration processes

> **Incident and problem management on the farm – Jim's experience**
> Growing up on a farm was my first introduction to incident and problem management. Harvest season was always stressful on the farm, as the crops needed to be brought in before winter weather made harvest difficult, and sometimes impossible. Much like IT today, farm machinery frequently broke down when we needed it most. Farmers are experts at 'fixing it fast' so the harvest can continue. Then, after the harvest was completed, farmers took the time to figure out why those equipment failures occurred and implement preventive actions to make sure that the equipment would not fail in the same way the following season.

We must focus on incident management first. By now you may be saying, 'I thought this publication was about problem management. Why do we need to be talking about incident management?' These two processes are strongly interdependent and must work together to quickly and permanently restore services. If we don't get incident management right, we won't get problem management right. They share common goals, objectives, process activities, data, information, and categorization and prioritization schemes.

We defined 'service' in Chapter 1, and said that problem management is one of two service resolution and service restoration processes. The other process is incident management.

The objectives of incident management are to restore IT services to normal operating levels as quickly as possible, to minimize service disruption and to ensure that agreed levels of service are maintained. In three words, incident management is 'restore it fast'. Incident management is responsible for logging, tracking and monitoring incidents and for ensuring compliance with the process to enable rapid restoration of service to the user.

> **Defining the levels of service**
> Note that normal operating levels and agreed levels of service should be defined within service level agreements (SLAs). An SLA is a signed agreement between the IT service provider and one or more customers describing the IT services that will be provided, service level targets for delivering those services, hours of service availability and support, and specific responsibilities of both parties.

The objectives of problem management are to minimize the impact of incidents when they occur, to proactively prevent the occurrence of incidents and to reduce and ultimately eliminate recurring incidents. In three words, problem management is 'fix and prevent'. Avoiding service disruptions through proactive problem management activities is a key

Problem Management

objective of problem management. It's true that incidents cannot always be prevented. For example, we cannot prevent hardware from failing. However, an important objective of problem management is to lessen the impact when such failures do happen. Problem management's primary objective is the identification of the underlying causes of incidents, thereby preventing recurring incidents and further service interruptions. While incident management's goal is to 'restore it fast', problem management may take considerable time to investigate the underlying cause and identify and implement a permanent solution to remove the error from the infrastructure.

Incidents are frequently reported to the IT organization through the service desk. One of the first activities that should occur is incident matching – checking to see if this incident has been reported before and if there is a workaround or a solution for it. If there is a documented workaround, apply the workaround and restore the service. If there isn't a workaround, investigate and diagnose the incident to determine a resolution. Whether or not the incident was resolved, and based on the criteria that your organization has established, it may be necessary to open a problem record or link the incident to a problem record. This is done so that problem management can determine the root cause, identify a workaround, and provide it to the service desk for use in resolving future similar incidents. When the root cause and a workaround have been identified, the problem is then called a known error. Problem management can then identify a permanent fix to prevent recurrence. Once a permanent fix has been identified, a request for change is submitted to change management to gain approval to implement the change. Depending

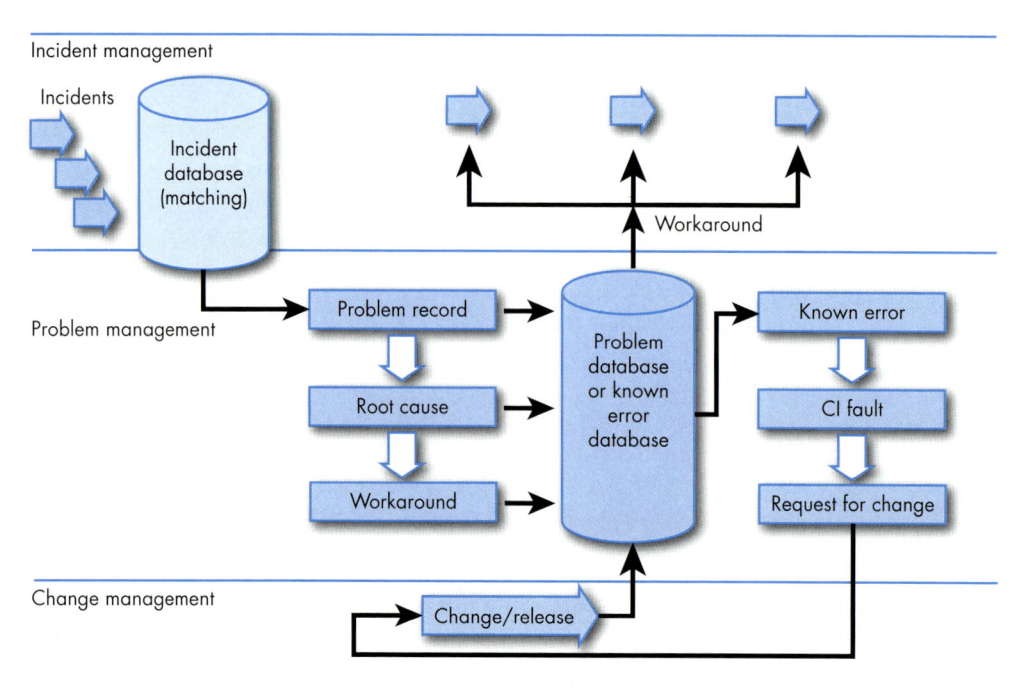

Figure 2.1 Process flow for restoring and fixing errors in the infrastructure

on the nature of the change, release management activities may be invoked to actually implement the change.

Figure 2.1 is a simple process swim lane diagram illustrating how incident management, problem management and change/release management processes all work together to quickly restore a service using workarounds, and then implement a permanent fix. We will come back to look at this diagram in more detail later in the chapter (Figure 2.6).

2.2 Why incident management must be effective

Even though incident and problem management are separate service management processes, there is a strong interdependency between them. This interdependency comes into play in a number of different ways. An incident may trigger the opening of a problem record and some of the information contained in the incident record may be copied to the problem record when it is first created. Examples of copied/shared information might be the summary or description of the incident, categorization information (such as the number of affected users, services and locations) and, initially, the problem record may take on the priority of the incident record that triggered it. Thus, problem management effectiveness is dependent upon carefully logged and categorized incident data.

Incident management:

- Logs data that is used for trending by both reactive and proactive problem management
- Categorizes incidents by customer, business unit and service, which is fundamental to obtaining meaningful metrics and understanding business impact
- Prioritizes incidents, which in turn aids in the prioritization of problem records
- Links incidents to problems, known errors or knowledge articles which help in understanding business impact and in the prioritization of the problem.

Note that an incident record is different from a problem record. An incident may trigger the opening of a problem record, but it will never become a problem record. They are separate entities.

2.3 The differences between incident and problem management

The following scenario illustrates the relationship and the differences between incident and problem management.

An incident occurred inside an IT organization's data centre. The computer room started heating up, temperature alarms started sounding, server fans increased to full speed and the data centre began experiencing power fluctuations as it was already operating at its maximum power capacity. The operations staff began performing incident management activities ('restore it fast'). Their goal was to assess the current situation and determine how best to restore normal service operation as quickly as possible. They needed to cool the computer room and minimize power fluctuations. Their goal was not to worry about the cause of the incident as problem management determines the cause at a later time. They quickly came up with a workaround, which was to unplug test servers, set up fans and run extension cords to bring in additional power from nearby rooms. The result was that the temperature and the power returned to acceptable levels. In other words, they restored the data centre to 'normal service operation'. Incident management was completed.

However, their workaround was not a long-term solution. What caused the incident in the first place? This is the realm of problem management ('fix and prevent'). Vendor investigation and diagnosis determined that a condenser had failed in one of the air-conditioning units. The operations team submitted an emergency change request to replace the condenser. The change was approved, the condenser replaced and the problem was fixed. However, from a problem management perspective there was still more work to be done! This type of failure could potentially happen again so they needed to take actions that would prevent this from reoccurring in the future (remember – problem management entails fixing **and preventing**). They decided to increase the frequency of the vendor preventive maintenance cycles on the air-conditioning units and to have this inexpensive part replaced with each maintenance cycle.

In summary, incident management restored the service to normal operation temporarily, while problem management restored the service to its usual and common state. All too often, we've seen organizations do one of two things with regard to incident and problem management:

- They perform incident management activities only and never perform problem management activities when needed, i.e. they never look for the root cause and apply a permanent fix to prevent the incident from occurring again.
- They perform incident and problem management activities simultaneously using the same limited resources, which means they try to find the root cause at the same time as trying to restore the service. Trying to do both simultaneously will delay restoration of the service, thus negatively impacting the productivity of the users.

Note that the scenario described above implies that incident management is always done prior to problem management. This is true sometimes, but not always. It depends on the amount of staff resources you have to work on incident and problem management. If you have enough resources, both processes can be executed concurrently. One set of resources is working on restoring service as quickly as possible while the other set of resources is working to determine root cause, a permanent fix and what can be done to prevent this from happening again. If you are limited in resources, always perform incident management first to get the service restored as quickly as possible, and then work on problem management activities.

Incident and problem management fundamentals

> **Note**
> If during diagnosis of an incident the root cause is discovered (not searched for) and it is apparent how to permanently fix the error, there is no need to open a problem record to engage problem management. Simply submit a request for change to change management (from incident management) to gain approval to implement the permanent fix.

2.4 Common goals and objectives

While incident and problem management are distinct processes, they do share some common goals and objectives. These are to:

- Improve availability of services
- Improve service quality
- Minimize the impact to the organization when incidents and problems do occur
- Improve customer satisfaction.

2.5 A summary of similarities and differences between incident and problem management

Table 2.1 summarizes the similarities and differences between incident and problem management, including some extra points not mentioned above.

Table 2.1 Similarities and differences between incident and problem management

Similarities	Differences
Share common goals, objectives and process activities	Incident management is focused on restoring service as quickly as possible ('restore it fast'), while problem management is focused on eliminating or minimizing errors in the infrastructure and preventing incidents from occurring ('fix and prevent')
Typically use the same categorization, impact and priority coding systems	
Often capture similar data (they will have separate records but these records should be linked)	
Use knowledge management best practices to facilitate the resolution of incidents or problems	While incident management may identify and implement a workaround to quickly restore a service, problem management has primary responsibility for identifying and documenting workarounds to reduce the time to restore service when incidents occur
Use structured problem-solving techniques	
	Incident management is reactive in nature, while problem management is both reactive and proactive
	Work related to incidents often begins at the service desk, while work related to problems often begins with personnel that have deeper levels of technical expertise

2.6 Common process activities between incident and problem management

Figure 2.2 shows a typical incident management process flow. It has 'swim lanes', which typically represent roles, down the left side. Single-sided rectangular boxes represent process activities. You will also see decision points represented by diamonds, double-sided rectangular boxes reflecting an interface to an external process, solid bars called transitional joins and directional arrows which indicate the process flow. Each of the shaded activities in this diagram is common (similar) between incident and problem management. Let's now look at each of those shared activities in more detail.

2.6.1 Identification and logging

An incident may be reported in several different ways: a user may place a call or send an email to the service desk, an incident may be recorded within your ITSM tool from the self-service portal, or your service desk may take walk-ins. Incidents may also be reported as a result of an 'elbow-grab' (a desktop support person is despatched to work on an incident at a user's desk and, while there, they are asked by another user to work on an incident that they are experiencing). Or, your system administrators may be identifying and detecting incidents as they monitor their technology domains.

Application and system monitoring tools may detect an event that has significance for your organization based upon the criteria and rules that have been established. Those same monitoring tools could automatically open an incident (or problem) record within your ITSM tool. If event management is set up correctly, this can facilitate the fastest possible detection and intervention by the IT service provider.

Regardless of when and how incidents are detected, all incidents should be logged and recorded. The purpose of logging is to provide an historical record of the impact and the level of effort required to restore service, and to optimize the use of support resources. Logging provides data that can be used:

- By both reactive and proactive problem management
- To facilitate trending and root cause analysis
- For creating and maintaining knowledge articles
- For training purposes
- For tracking progress towards resolution goals and compliance with the process
- For management reporting.

Logging enables access to critical information, such as description, symptoms and previous resolutions, which can be used by the support groups to more quickly restore service. An example of symptom codes and their meaning is provided in Appendix D. Table 2.2

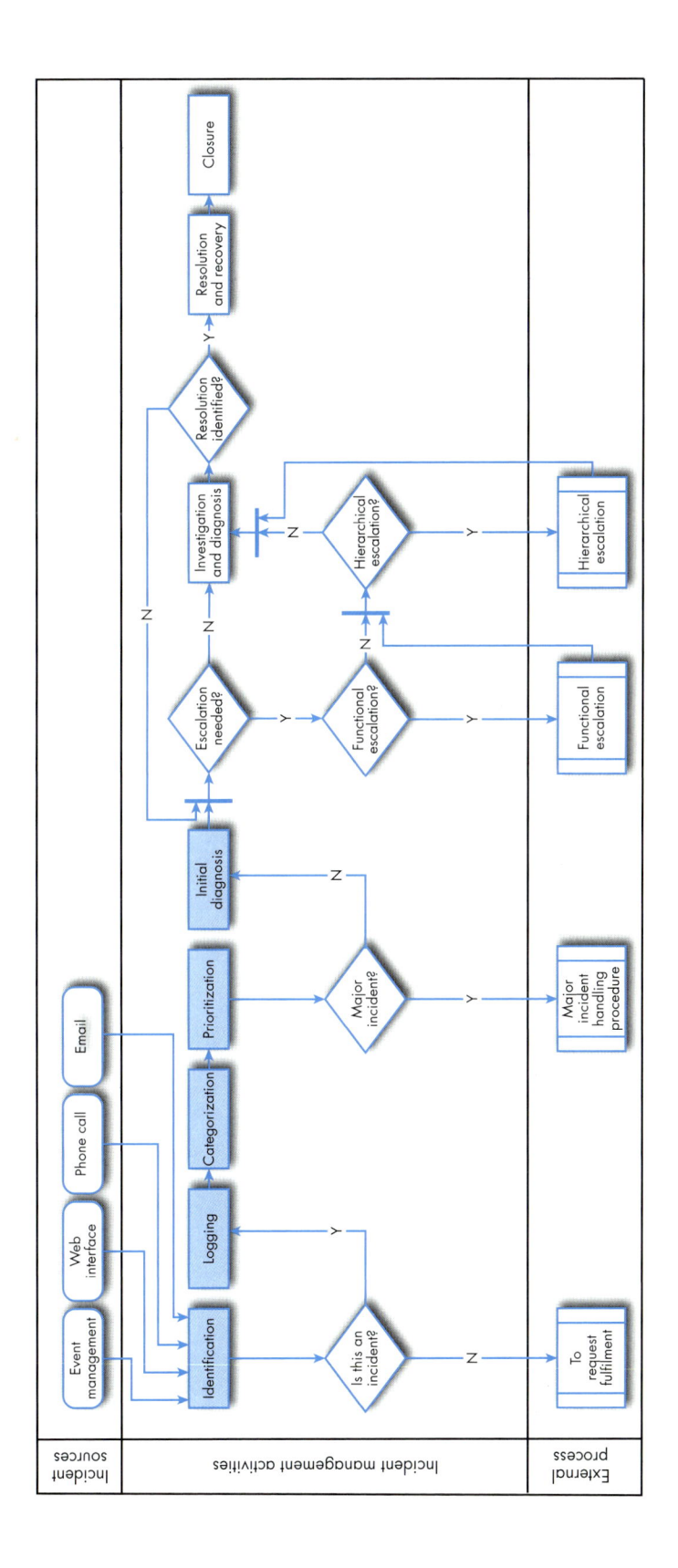

Figure 2.2 Incident management process flow

Table 2.2 Common data to capture when logging

Data item	Description
Record ID	A unique primary key for each record. Usually tool-generated and not editable
Created date	The date and time that the record was created. Usually tool-generated and not editable
Status	The status of the record. Represents the current state of the record in its lifecycle
Recorded by	The person who received the service call, or created the incident or problem record. Usually tool-generated and not editable
Detected by	How was the incident detected? Choices might be: user, system administrator or event management
Reported by	How was the incident reported? Choices might be: phone, email, self-service portal, walk-in or elbow-grab
Initiator	The person reporting the incident
Initiator information	Information that is useful to the service desk and support groups when working to resolve the incident quickly. This information is usually tool-generated and may include alias, telephone number, location, mail box, user ID, email address, job title and business unit
Summary	A description of the incident provided by the caller and the service desk
Description	Detailed information regarding the incident provided by the caller, service desk and/or support groups
Categorization information	Usually consists of major category and subcategory
Affected service	The service that has experienced a disruption, degradation or breakdown. If more than one service is affected, link the incident or problem record to each affected service configuration item record in the configuration management database
Symptom	An indication of the incident or problem. Symptoms are usually specific to the major category and subcategory combination
Configuration item	The configuration item that is associated with the service disruption and believed to be at fault
Impact	The business criticality of the incident which takes into account the number of affected services, business processes, users, financial loss etc.
Urgency	Urgency determines how quickly activities to restore service need to begin based on potential impact to the user or organization
Priority	The priority is derived from a combination of impact plus urgency. Often not editable
Assigned support group	The technical support group an incident or problem is assigned to. Used for functional escalation

Incident and problem management fundamentals

represents a subset of typical data that is captured and logged for reported incidents and/or problems. Note that data item names will vary based on the organization and the ITSM tools in use.

Table 2.2 includes 'detected by' when logging data. By recording this information, an IT service provider is able to determine if the incident management process is maturing. For example, less mature IT organizations will have more incidents detected by users and fewer detected by IT staff or by the event management process. Implementing ITSM best practices and supporting tools will result in having more incidents detected by IT staff and event management and a reduction in the number of incidents detected by end-users. Figure 2.3 demonstrates this desired relationship and trending as the organization matures. Obviously to trend this information, you must capture it.

The 'reported by' field is an additional way for an IT service provider to determine if its incident management process is maturing. As a service desk manager, you are always looking for ways to increase operational efficiency and reduce staffing costs. One strategy would be to implement alternative methods for the reporting and recording of incidents other than a phone call to the service desk. This is where options like self-service portals, submissions by email and system monitoring tools (event management) come into play. Effective communication and training on the organizational benefits and use of these options will reduce the number of incidents being reported by phone calls, walk-ins and elbow-grabs and lead to better management of staffing resources (see Figure 2.4).

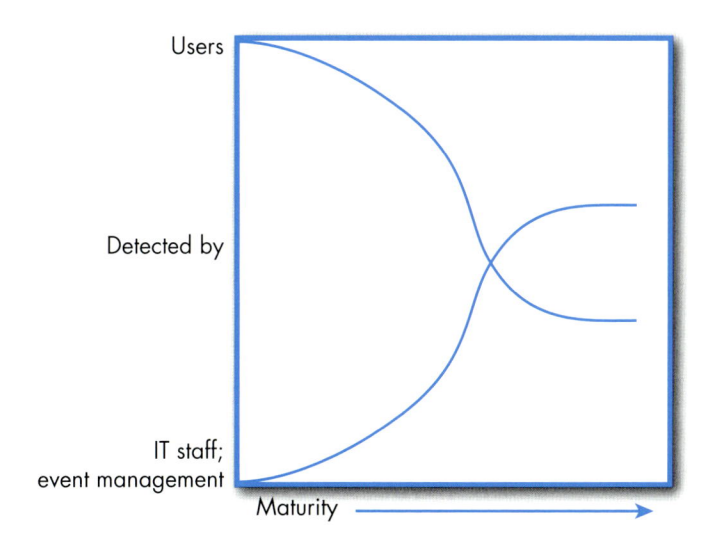

Figure 2.3 Trending 'detected by' over time

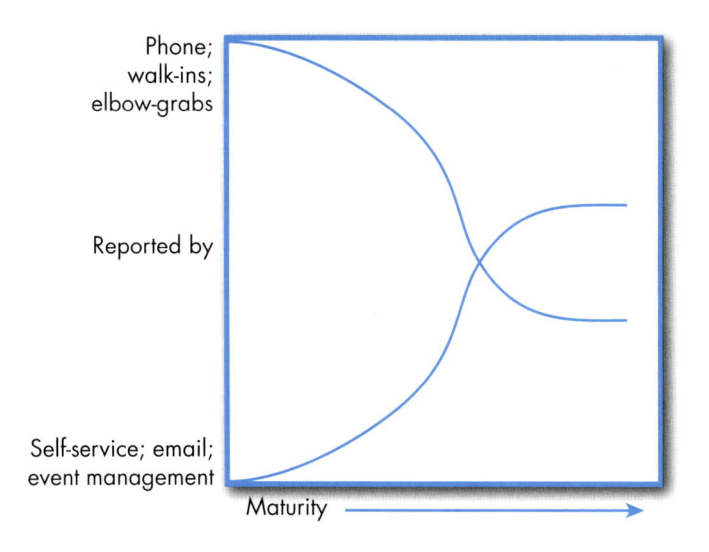

Figure 2.4 Trending 'reported by' over time

2.6.2 Categorization

Categorizing an incident or problem record is part of the data capture activity associated with logging. Categories are simply a way of classifying or naming a group of things that have something in common. Proper categorization is critical to both incident and problem management as it helps to determine the correct resources that need to be assigned. This information is also important for matching incidents to problem records, known errors and workarounds, for the prioritization of the record and for the accurate identification of trends and patterns.

There are a number of different categorization schemes in use within the IT industry, each having its own strong and vocal proponents. Every IT organization is different, so no one categorization scheme 'fits all'. An organization's categorization scheme is going to be dependent upon a number of factors: services provided, technology platforms in use, business and geographical make-up, process maturity and ITSM tool capabilities. In some organizations, the categorization scheme may be quite simple, while other organizations may use a multilevel categorization scheme. Figure 2.5 illustrates a simple, multilevel, three-tiered, technology-oriented categorization scheme.

In Figure 2.5, the top level represents a major category. In this example, the two major categories shown are hardware and software. Other examples of major categories might be network, facilities, telecom and storage. Next there can be multiple subcategories within a major category. For instance, within hardware there are servers, printers, workstations, monitors and so forth. In this example, we subcategorized this hardware incident as a server-related incident. Further categorization shows that we've determined the hard drive is the IT component or configuration item that is at fault. Regardless of how you design your

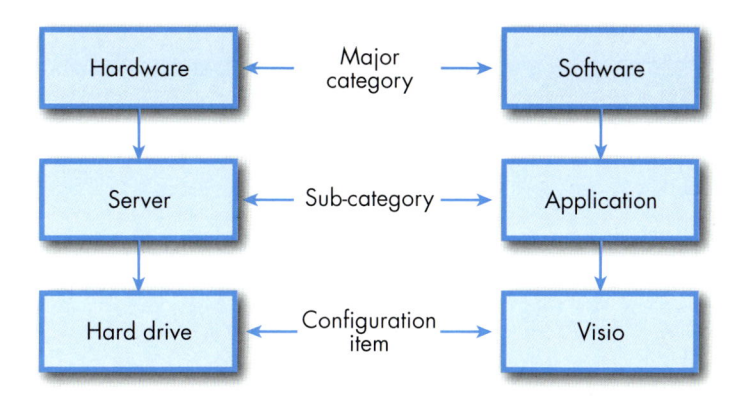

Figure 2.5 Example of a multilevel categorization scheme

categorization scheme, it is strongly recommended that at least the first two levels are common and shared between incident, problem, change and configuration management. A more detailed example of a two-tiered categorization scheme is provided in Appendix E.

Note that it is important to be able to record or report on initial categorization of the incident versus final categorization, as these may be different. As an example, a user calls into the service desk stating they cannot get to their email. Based on the symptoms relayed by the user, the service desk initially categorizes the incident as being a software/application incident related to the email service, with Outlook® as the specific application or configuration item at fault. Thus the incident record will initially be assigned to the Outlook applications team. Table 2.3 is an example of how this incident was initially categorized. Note that the affected service should be recorded and should be part of any categorization scheme.

Table 2.3 Initial categorization of an incident

Detected by	Reported by	Major category	Subcategory	Affected service	Configuration item	Assigned to	Priority
User	Phone	Software	Application	Email	Outlook	Applications	Medium

After investigation and diagnosis, the applications team concluded it was not an Outlook error because Outlook resides on two different servers and the application was running fine on the second server. They subsequently determined that one of the servers was down and the incident was reassigned to the Windows® engineering team for resolution. The Windows engineering team validated that one of the servers supporting the Outlook application was down and subsequently rebooted the server to bring it and the Outlook application back up. Users were then able to access their email. The final categorization of the incident is shown in Table 2.4.

Table 2.4 Final categorization of an incident

Detected by	Reported by	Major category	Subcategory	Affected service	Configuration item	Assigned to	Priority
User	Phone	Hardware	Server	Email	SRV123	Windows engineering	High

In this example, the initial categorization of the incident was different from the final categorization. There are two primary reasons why you would want to know that the initial and final categorizations are different. First, it would provide an opportunity for the service desk to meet with the first assigned support group to understand how they determined the incident was not theirs to resolve. It may be that the investigation techniques or scripts the assigned group used could be provided to the service desk. This would improve the service desk diagnosis and triage capabilities, and get the assignment of the incident to the right support group on the first attempt. Secondly, it is absolutely critical to problem management that when the incident is resolved the record reflects the final categorization of the configuration item that was at fault (or suspected to be at fault) and the steps taken to resolve the incident. Proactive problem management is dependent on complete, accurate and current information stored in incident records for its use in incident analysis and trending.

2.6.3 Prioritization

An IT organization is limited in the number of resources available to resolve incidents and problems. When multiple incidents and problems are open, an IT service provider must determine which ones to work on first. The 'priority' of an incident (or problem) reflects the organizational response required (i.e. the level of resource and effort applied to restore the service). In essence, it is the sequence in which an incident or problem is worked. Assigning the correct priority is also essential for triggering appropriate escalations. Problems should be prioritized to reflect the technical and business impact and urgency as defined and agreed to with the customers through service level agreements. Best practice recommends using the same prioritization scheme for both incident and problem management. In summary, prioritization is important:

- To ensure appropriate allocation of resources for responding to business needs
- To ensure consistent response to incidents and problems across technical support groups
- To ensure the required levels of effort for resolution and restoration are understood by service providers and customers
- To ensure higher-impact incidents and problems are addressed with a greater sense of urgency
- To aid in tracking and trending of incidents for proactive problem management.

Priority should be based on 'impact' and 'urgency', in essence: $P = I + U$.

Impact is a measure of the degree to which users or business processes have been affected. The following are considerations when assigning impact:

- The number of services, users and business processes affected
- The level of potential financial losses
- The effect on the business' reputation
- Possible regulatory and legislative breaches
- Risk to life or limb.

Urgency is how quickly activities to restore service need to begin based on the potential impact to the user or the organization. Items for consideration when determining urgency can include the following:

- Effect on operational productivity
- Lost revenue
- Time of day
- Time of week
- Time of month
- Time of year
- Season of the year.

Table 2.5 Example of an 'impact' level table

Impact levels			
1 Extensive	2 Significant	3 Moderate	4 Minor
Multiple IT services are unavailable	An IT service is unavailable	Any system or service that is degraded	Little to no operational impact – tasks may be more difficult to perform
An entire store or building is down	A Tier 1 critical application is severely degraded	Any system or service where its features are non-operational or unavailable	No systems or users are affected
A Tier 1 critical application is down or unavailable	A non-critical application is down or unavailable. There is, or will be, a significant financial or operational impact to the organization		

Table 2.6 Example of an 'urgency' level table

Urgency levels			
1 Immediate	2 Quickly	3 Soon	4 When possible
Productivity halted. User(s) are unable to work and no workaround is available	Productivity significantly impacted. There is an inconvenience to users, but a workaround is available, although the workaround may only provide partial relief	Productivity is degraded. There may or may not be a workaround available	Little or no productivity impact. Users may be inconvenienced, but a suitable workaround is available, or a delay in resolution is considered acceptable

Note that it is important to provide clear examples and guidance for determining the level of impact and urgency from which priority will be derived. Tables 2.5 and 2.6 provide examples of the kind of impact and urgency guidance that should be provided.

Most ITSM tools support multiple levels and values for impact, urgency and priority. Some organizations define five or more levels, while three and four levels seem to be the most common.

We stated earlier that priority is based on the combination of impact plus urgency. So let's see what this looks like in practice. Using the levels for impact and urgency provided in Tables 2.5 and 2.6, we can build a prioritization model as represented by Table 2.7.

Table 2.7 Example of a prioritization model

Major incident		Urgency			
		1 Immediate	2 Quickly	3 Soon	4 When possible
Impact	1 Extensive	1 Critical	1 Critical	2 High	3 Medium
	2 Significant	1 Critical	2 High	3 Medium	3 Medium
	3 Moderate	2 High	2 High	3 Medium	4 Low
	4 Minor	2 High	3 Medium	3 Medium	4 Low

Incident and problem management fundamentals

The left side of the table reflects increasing impact from 'minor' (bottom) to 'extensive' (top). The top of the table reflects urgency from 'immediate' (left) to 'when possible' (right). The 16 cells to the bottom right show the priorities, while the top left corner represents a major incident.

In this example, Table 2.7 has four different priority levels: critical (1), high (2), medium (3) and low (4). The priority of the incident or problem will be based on where impact and urgency intersect. If impact is moderate and the urgency is quickly, the priority is 'high' (or 2).

Note that priorities may change because problem management will be performing more in-depth investigation of the configuration items that are affected by the incident, resulting in a better understanding of the scope and impact on user productivity. Be sure to document the reason for the priority change within the incident or problem record. If a decision is made to decrease the priority of an incident, the customer/user should be consulted and agree with the change. Audit reports should be produced on priority changes and provided to management for subsequent monitoring and review to determine whether or not the priority changes adhere to process guidelines.

While the above guidance on how to assign the appropriate priority to incidents and problems appears to be purely quantitative, often there are other (qualitative) factors that can influence the setting of incident and problem priority. For instance, many organizations have special handling instructions when an incident or problem is reported for a 'VIP' (very important person). VIPs usually include senior executives within the business or IT, or whose functional role within the organization is deemed critical (e.g. a doctor within a hospital). In this case, if the nature of the incident normally warranted a priority 2 assignment, the priority would be escalated to 1.

You might be asking, 'Are there other reasons why the priority of a problem should be escalated?' The answer is 'yes'. Some organizations set resolution targets (by priority) for problems, as they do for incidents. Once a problem passes its resolution target, the priority is escalated (some organizations describe this as an increase in severity).

With a limited amount of resources to work on incidents and problems, the use of a priority scheme helps an IT service provider to establish the relative importance of which incidents and problems to work on. However, you should keep in mind that those same resources may also be working on service requests and projects, deploying a change, performing day-to-day operational activities, attending meetings, and so on. Thus, contentions may arise between these competing work activities (priorities) and there should be a well-defined communication path for technical support groups to present all the facts of the situation to the business, so that all parties can jointly work out what is best for the business and then adjust priorities as necessary.

2.6.3.1 Major incidents

Organizations should set clear criteria for defining and determining what constitutes a major incident. A major incident is above and beyond even a priority 1 (all major incidents are priority 1s, however not all priority 1s are major incidents). A major incident could be considered an 'all hands on deck' situation where you make every effort to get the incident resolved because it is having a significant adverse impact on the organization.

A separate procedure should exist for major incidents, characterized by shorter response times and a greater sense of urgency for action. A major incident team should be established, led by a major incident coordinator, and communications to users should occur as defined within service level agreements. In many IT organizations, the major incident coordinator is the incident manager, while in others the major incident coordinator may be the problem manager. This makes sense as the problem manager needs to be part of any major incident team and any information collected during a major incident should be documented and handed over to problem management for use in determining root cause and a permanent fix. Examples of when a major incident might be declared are listed below. They each can have a significant impact on the business:

- A virus, Trojan, worm, or malware outbreak
- An entire network segment supporting multiple locations is down
- Multiple applications or systems are down
- The data centre has lost power
- Multiple incidents with similar symptoms have the potential to collectively be considered to have an extensive impact.

Note that while the prioritization model represented in Table 2.7 is necessary, it may not be complete. Earlier we said that 'the priority of an incident (or problem) reflects the organizational response required (i.e. the level of resource and effort applied to restore the service)'. If this is true, then we should provide additional guidelines on what level of effort needs to be applied based on the priority. Table 2.8 is an example of additional guidance that should be provided to the technical support groups.

2.6.3.2 Escalation

Assigning the correct priority is essential for triggering appropriate escalations. As soon as it becomes clear that the service desk is unable to resolve the incident, escalation to the appropriate support group should occur. Table 2.9 provides an example of an escalation scheme for incident management.

Functional escalation is about getting additional personnel with higher skills or access privileges involved in restoring the service. Many IT organizations refer to their functional teams as tiers. Tier 1 personnel are often referred to as the service desk, while Tier 2 personnel

Table 2.8 Expected level of effort based on priority

Priority code	Expected effort level of response	Target acknowledgement response time[a]	Target ticket status update time[b]	Target communication status update time[c]	Target resolution time[d]	Target percentage resolved on time[e]
P1	An immediate and sustained effort using all available resources until resolved. On-call procedures are activated, and vendor support invoked if appropriate. Hierarchical escalation is invoked	15 minutes (Monday–Friday business hours, otherwise, 30 minutes)	Every 30 minutes	Every hour Automated notifications will go out on status updates	4 hours (around the clock)	90%
P2	Assigned staff members respond immediately, assess the current situation, and may interrupt other staff working on lower-level priorities and/or service requests to assist in a timely restoration	30 minutes (Monday–Friday business hours)	Every 2 hours	Every 2 hours Automated notifications will go out on status updates	8 hours (around the clock)	90%
P3	Assigned staff members respond using standard procedures and operating within normal supervisory management of current workload	2 hours (Monday–Friday business hours)	Every business day	Automated notifications will go out on status updates	3 business days	90%
P4	Assigned staff members respond using standard operation procedures as time allows within current workload	1 business day	Every 2 business days	Automated notifications will go out on status updates	5 business days	90%

a The time the assigned group has to acknowledge receipt of the ticket.
b The time interval the assigned group has to update the work information in the ticket.
c The time interval that the service desk has to provide an update on the ticket status to affected users.
d The total time from when IT becomes aware of the incident (i.e. ticket creation) to incident resolution and restoration of service to the user. Service may be restored either by a workaround or by a permanent solution.
e The percentage of incidents which are resolved within the priority time frames specified and agreed to within service level agreements.

Table 2.9 Escalation scheme based on incident priority

Priority code	1st functional escalation (service desk to Tier 2)	2nd functional escalation (Tier 2 to Tier 3)	1st hierarchical escalation	2nd hierarchical escalation	3rd hierarchical escalation
P1	At 10 minutes	At 1 hour	Occurs immediately and every hour thereafter to IT management (communication should include all managers in the assignee's upward chain of command)		
P2	At 10 minutes	At 2 hours	At 2 hours (to supervisor)	At 4 hours (to manager)	At 6 hours (to director or above)
P3	At 15 minutes	At 6 hours	At 6 hours (to supervisor)	At 12 hours (to supervisor)	At 18 hours (to manager)
P4	At 15 minutes	At 10 hours	At 10 hours (to supervisor)	At 20 hours (to supervisor)	At 30 hours (to manager)

are typically the junior-level staff within the technical support groups and Tier 3 personnel are the more senior staff.

Hierarchical escalation is about communicating to management either for informational purposes or to obtain their assistance in engaging additional resources.

2.6.4 Initial diagnosis, matching and workarounds

Initial diagnosis is investigating the incident and gathering diagnostic data. The goal is to understand and document the symptoms, what led up to the incident, the trigger events that might have occurred and what went wrong. This information, along with the categorization of the incident, is useful when performing incident matching – attempting to determine if this has occurred before and if there is a documented workaround or solution that can be applied in the resolution and recovery activity of incident management.

Matching is something both incident and problem management will perform by searching incident records, problem records, known error records and/or knowledge articles to determine if the incident has been reported by other users, or perhaps by system monitoring tools. If the incident has already been reported, the assignee should link this incident to the existing (or 'parent') incident record. Additionally, if problem management has provided a solution or a workaround, the solution or workaround should be used to resolve the incident at the service desk, if possible.

Let's look again at the high-level service restoration diagram (Figure 2.1), but this time from the perspective of workarounds and known errors (Figure 2.6).

Incident and problem management fundamentals

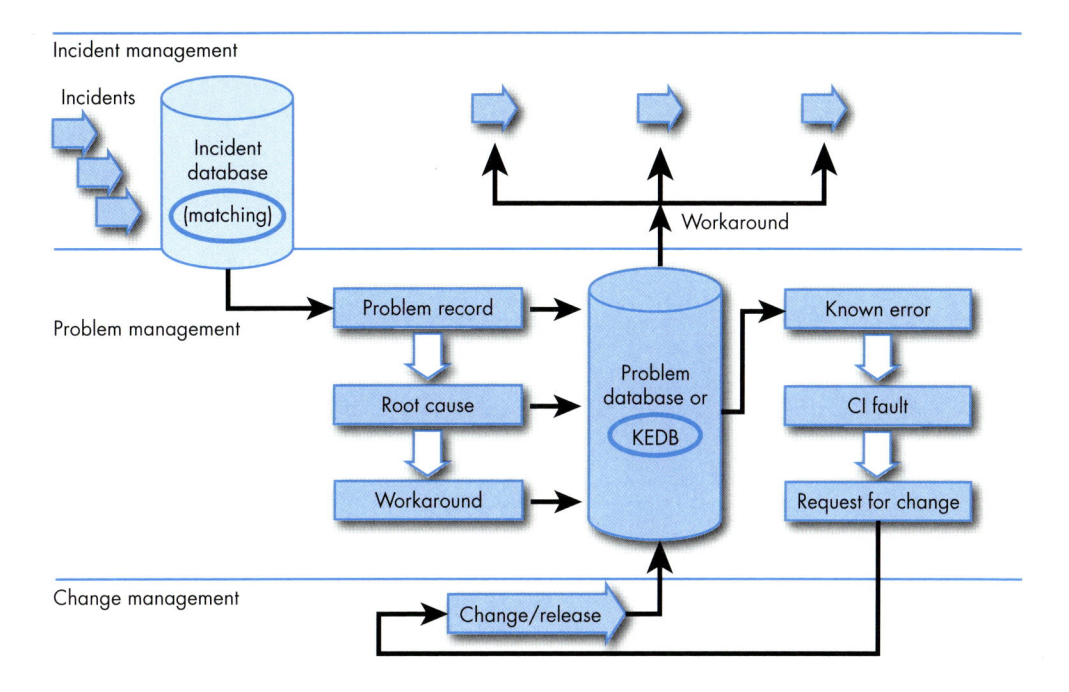

Figure 2.6 Incident matching and workarounds

When an incident first occurs, the ticket assignee should perform incident matching and search for existing incidents with similar symptoms to determine if the incident has been previously reported and if a workaround or solution is available. If a similar incident is found, and if a solution or workaround exists, apply it to the current incident and get the service restored as quickly as possible.

The assignee may also search the problem database, the known error database or the knowledge base to see if a workaround has been identified by problem management.

Workaround and known error access and retention will be based on process decisions your organization has made and the capabilities of your ITSM tool. Over the years, ITSM tool providers have caused confusion in the industry as to where to store workarounds (and permanent solutions) because their tool allowed (or in some cases required) the storage of a workaround in multiple different record types (and databases) including incidents, problems, known errors and solutions, in addition to a knowledge base. Ideally the workaround is stored in as few places as possible thus minimizing the additional effort required to keep all of the workaround sources current and reducing the confusion caused by not knowing where to look.

If matching does not return a possible workaround or solution, then the assignee should begin performing their own investigation and diagnosis to determine what the current situation is and how to resolve the incident.

While there are several other activities associated with the incident management process, those we have just reviewed are the activities common to both incident and problem management. Now that we have a proper foundation (incident management) in place, let's begin our in-depth look at problem management.

3 Problem management activities

> **Focus on the important things – Jim's experience**
> We often find that whatever we focus on has a tendency to improve and those things that we ignore have a tendency to degrade. This is certainly true in ITSM. Less mature organizations are focused on increasing the number of incidents resolved by the service desk (incident management) with little or no attention given to reducing the total number of incidents (problem management). How many times have we gone to a celebration honouring the IT staff who worked through the night to resolve a major incident, while those folks who work in problem management (to come up with a permanent solution) are never recognized? Less mature organizations have a tendency to focus only on those things that are urgent (incident management) while more mature organizations commit time and resources to those things that are important (root cause analysis and problem management). To paraphrase C. S. Lewis, whenever second things are prioritized over first things, the plan fails and not even the second things are obtained. If we put first things first, they are achieved and second things are picked up along the way. Problem management should be considered a first thing; it's about getting to the root cause of incidents, identifying permanent fixes and taking preventive action to keep the incident from happening again. It's time to change the way we are doing things.

Both Albert Einstein and William Deming are credited with the following definition of 'insanity'.

> *Insanity is doing the same thing over and over again and expecting different results.*

While it is obvious that change is often needed, many IT organizations remain unwilling to make changes, expecting instead to see improvements without changing the way they're doing business. Why continue to spend time and resources on resolving repeat incidents? Why don't we fix them permanently? That is the goal of problem management – getting to the root cause of incidents, identifying permanent fixes, and taking preventive action to keep the incident from happening again.

Let's begin our study of problem management with a simple illustration which shows the progression from an incident to the identification of the root cause. In Figure 3.1, we begin with an incident; there is a car sitting in the middle of the junction blocking traffic. This is not the 'normal operation' for traffic flow. To resolve the incident, the driver might get some help to push the car over to the side of the road, thus eliminating the blocking of traffic and restoring normal traffic flow. In this scenario, restoring normal traffic flow would mark the end of incident management.

But what's the underlying cause of this incident? We see the problem is that the car had stopped unexpectedly. The initial cause indicates the car is out of fuel. A deeper cause was that the car ran out of fuel because none was put in. The root cause is that there was no money for fuel because the fuel money had been spent on lottery tickets.

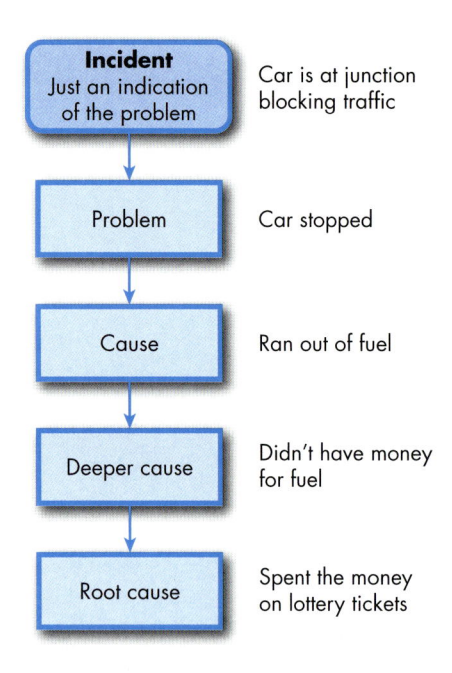

Figure 3.1 Relationship between an incident, problem and root cause

An incident is only an indication of a problem. Underlying every problem is a root cause. The root cause is the cause of an incident or problem to which a fix may be applied to resolve or prevent recurrence of the incident.

Remember that there are two main aspects of problem management – reactive and proactive. Reactive problem management is focused on solving problems in response to one or more incidents as they occur. Proactive problem management is focused on identifying and solving problems and known errors that might otherwise be missed; looking for trends and patterns; learning about known errors from external sources; and solving problems before incidents occur or reoccur.

Figure 3.2 is a broad overview of the problem management process showing inputs, major activities and outputs.

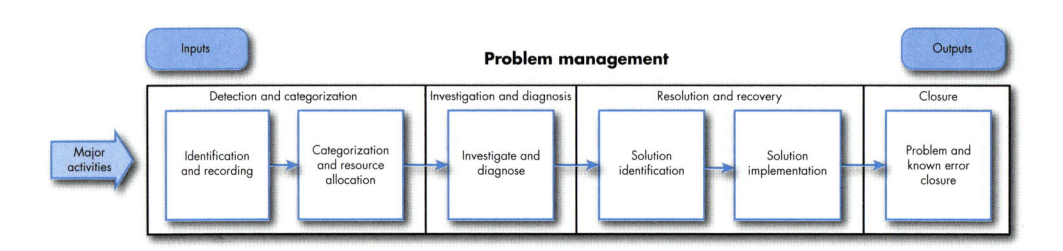

Figure 3.2 Major categories and activities of problem management

Let's spend a moment to look at some of the problem management inputs and outputs. You can see from the list below that problem management receives inputs from a number of different sources.

Inputs into problem management include:

- Incident records
- Incident reports
- Configuration management database (CMDB) and configuration item (CI) information
- System and monitoring logs
- Knowledge base article reuse counts (useful for trending by proactive problem management in identifying recurring incidents)
- Known error database (the number of incidents linked to known errors can assist in prioritizing problem management activities)
- Output from risk analysis activities
- Capacity data
- Change records
- Service level agreements
- Known errors from suppliers.

The most obvious input source is incident management, which is why we dedicated an entire chapter to making sure we have a solid understanding of the incident management process prior to beginning problem management. We also see from the list below that several of the problem management process outputs feed back into incident management.

Outputs from problem management include:

- Workarounds
- Known errors
- Permanent fixes
- Requests for change
- Closed problem and incident records
- Key performance indicator (KPI) and management reports
- Training recommendations
- Resource requirements for resolution options
- Communication requirements.

Figure 3.3 shows the major activities for problem management (refer to Appendix C for a detailed workflow of the major activities). You will notice that several of the major activities are shaded in the figure, indicating that those activities are common or similar between incident and problem management, thus once again underlining the importance of getting incident management right.

One final thought before we begin our investigation into problem management is that, given the complexity of this process as seen in Figure 3.3, it is important to be able to know the state of the problem record as it changes throughout its lifecycle. These different states allow reporting to occur that will indicate if the problem has been assigned, is being worked on, whether root cause and/or a workaround have been identified, and when the problem has been resolved. Table 3.1 reflects the more common states that a problem record may be set to throughout its life.

Table 3.1 Common states of a problem record

Problem record status	Description
Open or new	Initial status for a problem record, prior to assignment to a technical support group
Acknowledged	The record is in a technical support group work queue but work has not yet started
Cancelled	The record was cancelled without resolution or the record was opened in error
In progress	The record is assigned and being worked on by a technical support group member
Pending vendor	The record is pending a vendor or third-party action or response
Known error	The root cause and a workaround have been identified
Pending change	The record is pending the implementation of the workaround or permanent fix
Resolved	The permanent fix has been applied
Closed	The solution has been implemented in production, the solution has been validated as having solved the problem, and the quality and content of the data contained within the problem or known error record are adequate

Now that we have a solid foundation to build upon, let's begin our in-depth study of the problem management activities, beginning with detection and categorization.

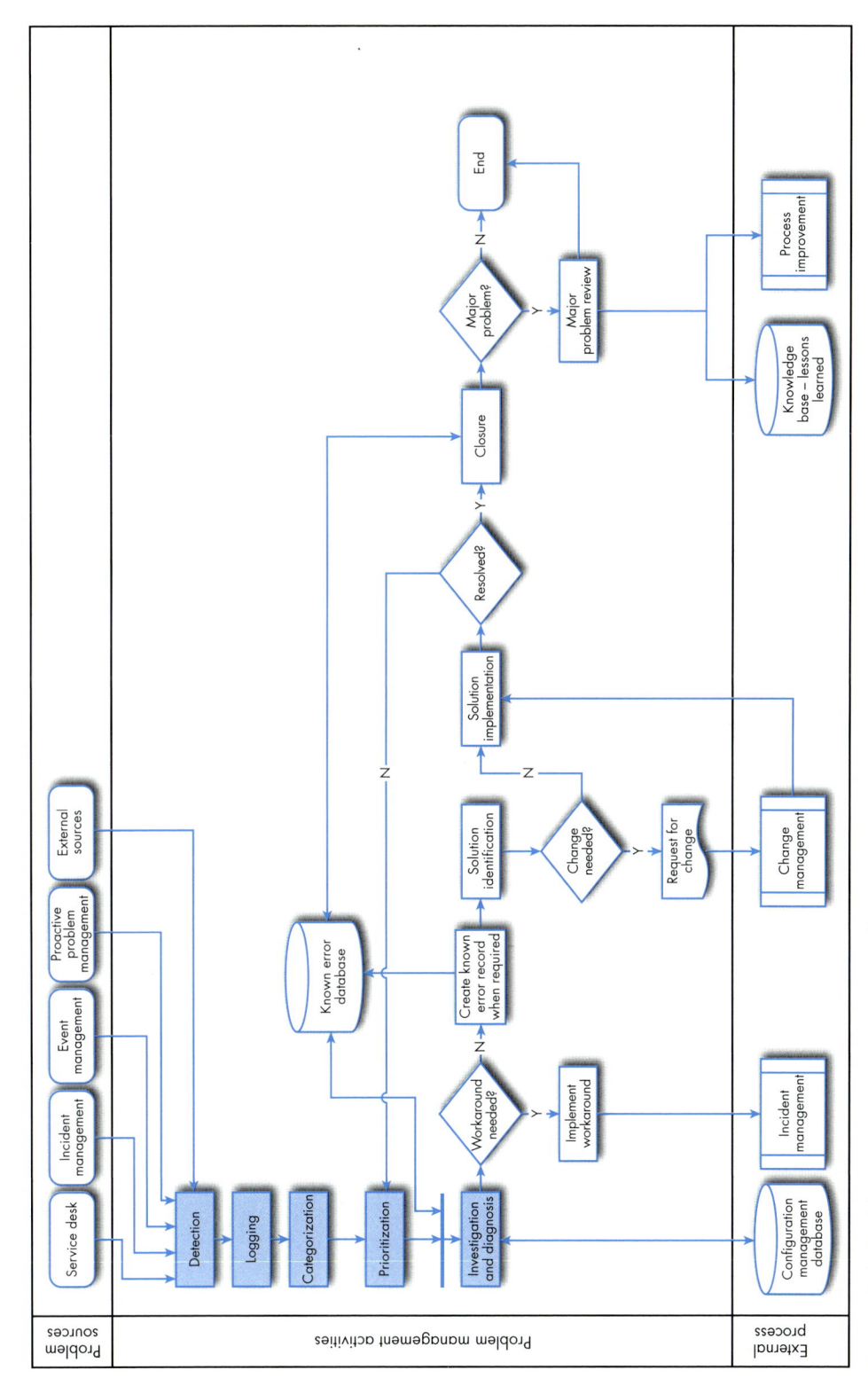

Figure 3.3 Problem management process flow

3.1 Detection and categorization

The first major category of problem management activities is called detection and categorization. It includes the activities of problem detection, logging, categorization and prioritization. As we see from Figure 3.3, problem sources include:

- The service desk
- Incident management
- Event management (from automated monitoring tools)
- Proactive problem management activities
- External sources (such as suppliers, contractors and service partners).

3.1.1 Detection

There are several triggers for the opening of a problem record. Table 3.2 provides examples of the more common triggers for both reactive and proactive problem management activities.

Table 3.2 Reactive and proactive triggers for opening a problem record

Reactive triggers for opening a problem record	Proactive triggers for opening a problem record
There is an incident for which the root cause is not known	Analysis of incidents over differing time periods reveals a recurring trend, indicating a problem might exist
The service desk suspects an incident may recur after initial resolution	Analysis of the IT infrastructure (by category, CI type etc.) by technical support groups identifies a potential problem
Analysis of an incident by a technical support group reveals a potential underlying problem	
Event and alerting tools automatically create a problem record due to fault detection	Analysis results from data and knowledge mining of the knowledge base
A major incident has been declared	Announcements of known errors from applications development or release and deployment teams
An emergency change has been submitted for an unreported incident	
	Reports generated from application or system software
	Service review meetings with customers
	Supplier review meetings
	Notification from a supplier that a problem or known error exists in their service or product

3.1.1.1 Proactive problem management

Having already completed our in-depth study of the incident management process, we now have a solid understanding of those reactive triggers for opening a problem record. So let's now spend some time looking at triggers for opening a proactive problem record.

Proactive problem management begins with the collection and review of various sources of data and information related to incidents and faulty CIs to determine trends and patterns that may expose weaknesses or fragility in the infrastructure, or to identify errors that have not yet been discovered. The focus is broader than just a single incident or problem. It looks out across the various technology domains and evaluates all available data, including incidents, problems, known errors, change records, configuration data, monitoring data, capacity data and even supplier data and databases, looking for potential sources of service disruption. The objective of this effort is to spot trends and patterns, sometimes between seemingly non-related entities.

The configuration management system and CMDB can be a valuable source of information for proactive problem management. Trends and patterns can include looking at specific CI, incident or problem categories; an unusual number of incidents for a particular CI, location, line of business, software or technology; or an unusual number of changes to a CI or category of CIs. For example, a search of the CMDB could be performed and a report created showing all CIs that have had multiple incidents logged against them during a specific reporting period. This could be an indication of fragile CIs within the computing environment and may be an indication of an underlying problem.

Proactive problem management is reliant upon complete, accurate and available information. Thus, a focus on identifying and using validated sources of data is critical for the effective proactive assessment of the computing environment and for the service provider to produce business value from the proactive tasks. The knowledge gained from the proactive assessment of the technology domains should not be limited to just IT, but should be available to customers, suppliers and service partners involved in, or the recipient of, problem management activities.

Note that the first item in Table 3.2 under the proactive column states, 'Analysis of incidents over differing time periods reveals a recurring trend, indicating an underlying problem might exist'. This analysis does not necessarily need to be done by a person residing within a technical support group. If you have an analytical service desk agent who is good at running reports and analysing data, they could perform the initial analysis of incidents. If there is an indication of an underlying problem, they could then refer their findings to the technical support groups for further investigation and diagnosis.

It is important to commit resources to proactive problem management as it moves an organization from a fire-fighting and reactive organization to a more thoughtful organization where services are improved, not just restored. In larger organizations, a number of support personnel should be dedicated to proactive problem management, while in smaller organizations this work may be accomplished by committing a percentage of support staff's time to proactive problem management activities. Another approach might be to have the problem manager perform proactive problem management activities, while technical support staff will focus on reactive problem management. We will address these options in more detail in Chapter 5.

3.1.2 Logging

We previously defined a problem as the underlying cause of one or more incidents (or potential incidents) whose root cause is usually not known. If this definition were to be applied strictly, then a problem should be opened for every incident that occurs for which the root cause is not known, but this is not practical or achievable in most organizations. Do you really want to take the time and expend the resources to open a problem record, find the root cause and a permanent fix for all incidents whose root cause is not known and for any incident priority level? Keep in mind that if you're going to expend resources on investigation and diagnosis of a problem, you will likely expend those resources again to find a permanent solution.

3.1.2.1 Logging (when)

When first implementing a formal problem management process, the technical staff are often hesitant and unsure as to when to open a problem record, so few get opened. Thus, a clear list of the criteria for when a problem record must be opened is a great place to begin. The following list is a suggested starting point for when to open a problem record:

- Any incident that is assigned a priority 1 or where a major incident has been declared
- Multiple incidents showing the same symptoms
- Alarms from monitoring devices that are deemed high impact
- Notification from a supplier that a problem or known error exists in their product or service
- Any incident that is opened as a result of a security event (e.g. viruses).

When to open a problem record is dependent on a number of factors. Initially you may decide that you should only open a problem record for priority 1 and 2 incidents. Or maybe you open a problem record for any priority incident for which you don't know the root cause but you only investigate priority 1 and 2 problems until you reach a more stabilized environment. Later, you may decide to allocate resources to investigate priority 3 and 4 records. It really depends upon the organization, the amount of resources available to expend on problem management, the number of problem records that are currently open (especially those of higher-level priorities), whether you think the incident may recur, the impact of the incident should it recur and a number of other factors.

3.1.2.2 Logging (who)

A problem record can be logged by the service desk, IT operations, event management or any technical support group member. The problem record should be opened by whoever first discovers or suspects that a problem may exist. From a reactive problem management perspective, an incident record must be opened first and the incident record linked to the problem record. There is much industry debate as to whether the service desk should be allowed to open a problem record. We believe they should, but under the following conditions or criteria:

- A clear definition of what constitutes a problem has been established within the organization
- Detailed problem management process training has been provided to the service desk agents
- The opening of a problem record is limited to experienced or lead service desk agents.

Given the above criteria, there is no reason why the service desk should not open a problem record and assign it to an appropriate technical support group. We haven't talked yet about specific problem management process roles and responsibilities (see Chapter 5), but one of the control points within a mature problem management process is that the problem manager or problem queue manager should review all opened problem records for their team and ensure that each one meets the definition of a problem, is not a duplicate record and belongs to their team for investigation and diagnosis. If any of these are false, the record should be appropriately updated with comments and the record cancelled or reassigned.

If the record has been opened appropriately, the problem manager or problem queue manager should then assess the problem and decide on the skills required to determine the root cause, identify an appropriate and available resource(s) to work on the problem and then assign the record to the appropriate team member.

3.1.2.3 Logging (tool considerations)

Logging problems is a very similar activity to logging incidents. Many of the more mature ITSM tools will allow you to create a problem record from an existing incident record and will automatically link that incident to the created problem record. When this happens, much of the information contained within the incident record is copied into the newly opened problem record. This information might include how it was detected or reported; the assigned support group; the priority of the problem; the incidents or events that triggered the problem; which users, services and equipment are affected; and the details of any diagnostic or attempted recovery actions taken to date. An ITSM tool that facilitates the linking of data between event, incident, problem, change and configuration records can be a significant contributor to process efficiency.

3.1.3 Categorization and prioritization

As mentioned earlier, categorization and prioritization schemes should be shared between incident and problem management, or at the least, be very similar. This will facilitate:

- Understanding the business impact, which in turn can be used to determine prioritization and whether to proceed with problem investigation and diagnosis
- Effective use of problem management resources
- More accurate trending
- More effective incident and problem matching
- Understanding the true nature of the problem by easily tracing the problem back to the incident(s) that triggered it
- Capture of data that can be used for reporting on critical success factors and key performance indicators.

3.2 Investigation and diagnosis (root cause analysis)

The next major activity in the problem workflow is investigation and diagnosis. The purpose of investigation and diagnosis is to determine what happened, determine why it happened (understanding the causal factors), identify and document a workaround (when necessary) and determine the root cause. The ideal outcome of this activity is to move the 'problem' to a 'known error' (where root cause and a workaround have been identified).

3.2.1 Control points

These are points in the process flow where key decisions must be made or actions taken. One of the problem management process control points is a determination as to whether to proceed with investigation and diagnosis given time requirements and resource constraints. Thus a reassessment of the impact, available resources and cost of pursuing the root cause should be made at this point by both the business and IT staff. It may be decided that it is not worth pursuing. If so, documentation of this decision should be made within the problem record and the record should be closed with an appropriate closure code.

3.2.2 Matching

Assuming determination of the root cause will be pursued, one of the first actions taken should be to perform matching. Although matching was performed when the incident was first created, problem management should perform it again and search incidents, the problem database, the known error database or the knowledge base to see if a solution or workaround exists. Individuals within an IT organization have their own unique knowledge and experience, different analytical skills and different ways of searching knowledge. It is therefore possible that technical support group members will use additional search criteria that will enable them to identify a documented solution or workaround when incident management did not. The technical support member may also have access to service partner and supplier technical databases where they can conduct searches. Thus, all problem record assignees should be expected to search and review any existing workarounds and solutions. The goal is to reuse a solution whenever possible.

3.2.3 Investigation and diagnosis team

There are times when investigation and diagnosis will simply be an individual effort. However, more complex problems or problems that have a high impact and high visibility within the organization will require the forming of a cross-functional team that will work together to determine the root cause.

To form the team, you first need to understand the nature of the problem so you can determine who should be involved. The team might consist of technical subject matter experts from various functional teams such as hardware, software, applications, network, database and/or security teams. The team may also include customers, service owners and management. The optimal team will have complementary skills, be committed to achieving the goals and objectives, and hold each other mutually accountable.

The problem manager should typically act as a facilitator who leads the team to the identification of root cause and keeps the team on target. The problem manager should solicit and encourage participation and feedback and come prepared to the meeting with as much information as possible about the problem.

3.2.4 Six steps

Table 3.3 lists the six steps to be taken during the investigation and diagnosis along with a brief description of each step.

Table 3.3 The six steps involved in investigation and diagnosis

Steps involved in investigation and diagnosis		Description
1	Define the problem	Define the problem in terms of what took place, where it is occurring (and where it is not occurring), when it occurred (timeline) and significance (impact; frequency)
2	Identify a workaround	Update the known error database or knowledge base with any workaround that is found, or with any new information that would be meaningful to add to an existing known error record or knowledge article
3	Collect data	Collect data that can support or point to the causal factors resulting in the problem
4	Analyse the data and identify possible causes	Look for causes in actions and conditions and identify how causes interact with one another
5	Identify the root cause	The root cause is a cause to which you can attach a solution to resolve or prevent recurrence
6	Document the analysis done to reach the conclusion	Support and document your conclusion with evidence

Step 1: Define the problem

Every problem investigation and diagnosis activity should start with a well-defined problem. All too often we see an incident or problem description that looks similar to the following:

Can't access patient records.

What does this really tell us? The obvious answer is – not much. This is an example of a poor problem definition. A much better problem definition would look like the following:

The network segment connecting the main office to the hospital went down at 1.12 a.m. on the 4th of June affecting all staff and IT services at the hospital.

Additional questions that may help when defining a problem are listed in Table 3.4.

Table 3.4 Questions to ask when defining a problem

What?	Where?	When?	Significance
What service, CI, business unit or customer group is being affected?	Where is the problem occurring now? (location – where is it and where is it not occurring)	When were symptoms first seen or the problem first seen? (day and time)	How often is the problem occurring? (Is its frequency diminishing, staying the same, getting worse?)
What are the symptoms?	Where was the problem first seen in the operational process cycle?	When was the change made that may have initiated the problem?	How many services, CIs, business units or customer groups are being affected?
What change(s) was (were) made on or around the time the symptoms started? (Consider people, process and technology changes)	Where have there been other manifestations of this problem?	When in the operational processing cycle was the problem first seen?	How significant is the impact on resources such as money, people, infrastructure, applications and other resources?
What was the reason for the change(s)?		When have there been additional manifestations of the problem?	
What other things were occurring or running at the same time as the symptoms of the problem?			

Step 2: Identify a workaround

Workarounds and known errors are developed by problem management and are used to reduce the time to restore services. Workarounds are provided to the service desk and others in order to resolve the current and future similar incidents.

In Chapter 1 we defined a workaround as a temporary method of reducing or eliminating the impact of an incident until a permanent solution is available. Although it is a primary responsibility of problem management to identify and store a workaround, other processes and functions may also identify and document a workaround. In practice, it is often incident management that identifies a workaround during incident resolution and documents the workaround within the incident record or within a knowledge base article. For example, if a user calls the service desk stating they are unable to print to the network printer next to them, the agent might decide to reroute the user to a different network printer so they can print their current and future documents until problem management identifies the root cause and comes up with a permanent fix. The rerouting to a different network printer is an example of a workaround identified and documented by incident management.

When problem management identifies a workaround, we recommend another control point be designed into the process. Its purpose is to review/validate the proposed workaround. An appropriate member of a technical support group should identify and test the proposed workaround before it is made available for widespread use to ensure that it will work, that it is efficient and that it is the most cost-effective workaround available. This review would typically be part of the role of a problem manager or problem queue manager.

In addition to restoring services quickly, there are several other advantages to identifying and documenting workarounds. Having workarounds available can result in a reduction in the number of emergency changes. When we incur a service outage we understandably want to get the service restored as quickly as possible, which can increase the number of emergency changes. Emergency changes can introduce risk to our production environment because we don't always take time to test the change, communicate the change, or develop a back-out plan in case something goes wrong. If a workaround is available to restore the service, we have bought ourselves more time to identify, test and communicate the permanent fix, and subsequently we can submit a normal change rather than an emergency change to change management. Having workarounds available should also result in a reduction in the time required for new service desk staff to become effective at resolving incidents and a reduction in the number of escalations to Tiers 2 and 3 support groups.

> **Using workarounds indefinitely**
> Workarounds may be used indefinitely when the cost of a permanent fix outweighs the benefits of a permanent solution. In essence, a workaround could become the 'permanent fix' because the time, effort and cost to resolve the incident permanently may outweigh the benefits of continuing to use the workaround. The decision to use the workaround indefinitely is not solely an IT decision. It is a business decision. The business should be consulted with the options and alternatives and asked to make a decision as to whether to continue using the workaround or to pursue a permanent fix.

When the root cause of a problem is known and a workaround has been identified, the problem becomes a known error. Known errors are stored in the known error database or knowledge base (as a knowledge article) and are used to resolve incidents and restore service quickly should future similar incidents occur. Known error records and knowledge articles are searchable, reusable and structured objects that contain workarounds or resolutions primarily used by incident management.

The knowledge management system or organizational knowledge base is used in some organizations as the basis of the known error database. Alternatively, the known error database might be used as the basis for a knowledge base. How the information is stored is very important as it must be searchable and accessible. ITSM tools can facilitate and aid in knowledge management and matching. A good service support practice is to have the solution readily available to the service desk and first-line responders. Also, when appropriate, the solution may be made available to the end-user.

As the problem management process matures, the amount of information stored in the known error database or knowledge base should grow, and the organization should see a reduction in the time it takes to restore services and in escalations to Tier 2 and Tier 3 support groups. If these trends do not occur, then a detailed review of the database and surrounding activities should be undertaken to identify improvement opportunities.

Step 3: Collect data

There are numerous sources of data that pertain to a problem, including the following:

- Information gathered from interviews with the service desk, users and IT staff
- Incidents related to the problem
- System/application activity logs and journals
- Voicemails and emails
- Changes that may have been made to the suspected CI(s) at fault or to the overall computing environment
- Actions taken to date
- Documentation collected by the service desk and/or from operations at or before shift changes.

If possible, system/application activity logs and journals should be preserved (by incident management) before taking any corrective action when attempting to restore the service, as the data may prove to be critical in identifying the root cause.

Step 4: Analyse the data and identify possible causes

Once the data has been collected, analysis of the data should be conducted to help in determining root cause and understanding impact. We need to identify causes in actions and conditions and how these causes interact with one another.

Consider the following scenario.

> **Scenario**
> A man decides to drive in a blizzard at night to the nearest grocery store to pick up some chocolate ice cream. Visibility is limited and the roads are packed with ice and snow. While driving, he receives a text message, takes a moment to read it, and begins to answer it. He looks up momentarily and all of a sudden he sees a car stopped right in the middle of the road with no lights on. He immediately slams on the brakes, but it's too late. His car begins to skid sideways towards the stopped vehicle and the inevitable happens – he runs into the back of the vehicle in front of him. After checking himself and the other driver for injuries, the other driver explains that the reason his car was stopped in the middle of the road was because his alternator had stopped working and he had lost electrical power.

For the above scenario, the causes in actions are:

- Driving (when not really necessary)
- Driving too fast (based on weather conditions)
- Texting while driving
- Slamming on the brakes instead of pumping them.

And for the same scenario the causes in conditions are:

- Blizzard
- Limited visibility
- Roads packed with ice and snow
- Car stopped in middle of road
- Car had no lights
- Alternator failed.

Step 5: Identify the root cause

Causality has to do with the relationship between two different events; the first event being the cause and the second event being the effect of the cause. In essence, you're trying to determine what caused this effect.

At the beginning of this chapter, we used Figure 3.1 to show that there can be causes, deeper causes and ultimately a root cause to every problem. We went on to define root cause as the cause of an incident or problem to which you can apply a fix to resolve or prevent recurrence.

One of the key points we need to make now is that when we are looking to fix a problem permanently, we need to be careful to fix the root cause and not the symptoms of the problem. Referring back to Figure 3.1, if we put fuel in the car that would fix the problem (i.e. the car would be mobile again). But doing that would not have fixed the root cause, and therefore this problem could occur again. However, if we fix the gambling problem (the root cause), we should have money available for fuel that we can put into the car that should keep it from stopping in the first place. So bear in mind, when looking for a root cause, if fixing the cause you have settled on will not prevent recurrence, you have not found the root cause.

Root causes will usually fall into one of four classifications:

- Physical causes – components failed
- System errors – software failed
- Human causes – people did something wrong or failed to do something they should have
- Organizational causes – a process, policy or procedure is in error.

One could argue that there is a fifth classification of root causes – environmental. This is where natural events and weather-related causes affect services. While these natural events may indeed be the root cause of service disruptions, these events are usually outside our control. We should not undertake root cause analysis on those things which are outside of our control to effect resolution. The goal in identifying root cause is to ultimately lead us to a permanent fix. We can't fix nature, but we can mitigate and minimize its physical, system, human and organizational effects.

When looking for the root cause, and in addition to the four classifications listed above, it is helpful to keep people, process and technology in mind. Was this problem caused by a person? Was a process in error or not followed? Could the technology be at fault? Or could the problem have been caused by a combination of these?

Identifying the root cause can sometimes be challenging; thus establishing and using effective root cause analysis techniques is critical to successful problem management. Some of the more common techniques are described below in section 3.2.5.

Step 6: Document the analysis done to reach the conclusion

Once the root cause has been identified, it is important to document how you (or the investigation and diagnosis team) reached your conclusion. This information can be recorded in a standard template that is attached to the problem record, or in the problem record itself. The recorded information should include the following:

- Root cause analysis techniques used
- Data used in the analysis
- Sources of the data
- Systems, tools and personnel involved
- Possible causes that were considered and why they were ruled out
- The root cause and the actions taken to prove the cause.

3.2.5 Root cause analysis techniques

As we noted in Step 5 above, root cause analysis (RCA) is critical to successful problem management. Fortunately, there are tried and proven RCA techniques to help us get to the root cause. The following sections provide an introduction to seven of the more common techniques and include examples of the techniques in practice.

The seven techniques are:

- Five Whys
- Brainstorming
- Chronological analysis
- Ishikawa diagrams
- Pareto analysis
- Kepner–Tregoe
- Fault tree analysis.

3.2.5.1 Five Whys

This is a simple technique where repeatedly asking 'Why?' will help us get to the underlying contributing factors or root cause.

> **Using the technique with teenagers**
> Teenagers are familiar with this technique. Parent – 'Why have your grades dropped this term?' Response, 'I haven't had time to do all of the homework.' Parent – 'Why haven't you had time to do your homework?' Response, 'I have so many things on my schedule each week.' Parent – 'Why has your schedule changed since last term?' The questioning continues until together you are able to identify contributing factors and/or the cause.

Beginning with a clear definition of the problem, identify what event took place and for each event, ask 'Why' that occurred. While it is certainly possible to ask 'why?' beyond five times, there is usually a diminishing value in continuing.

While the Five Whys technique is not particularly scientific, it is fairly quick and easily explained. This technique is recommended for problem management teams that are just getting started as it is the simplest RCA technique to use for identifying the root cause on minor problems.

> **Note**
> The investigator needs to be careful not to stop at symptoms, but instead dig deeper, looking for lower-level causes.

> **Another example of the Five Whys technique**
> Problem statement – The air-conditioning unit stopped functioning in the data centre.
>
> *Why?*
>
> The condenser stopped working.
>
> *Why?*
>
> It was old and was never replaced.
>
> *Why?*
>
> We have no preventive maintenance contract with the vendor.
>
> *Why?*
>
> The maintenance contract was not submitted for renewal during the last budget cycle.
>
> *Why?*
>
> The person responsible for submitting the contract left the company and their duties were not reassigned.
>
> This is a simple scenario, but a good example of the use of this technique. Looking at the conclusion we arrived at, if responsibility for submitting the maintenance contract for renewal had been assigned, it probably would have been renewed (as it had been in previous budget cycles), and the aging condenser would have been replaced as part of regular maintenance, thus preventing a failed condenser that caused the air-conditioning unit to stop functioning.

3.2.5.2 Brainstorming

This is an unstructured technique that uses the knowledge of various personnel to identify potential causes and solutions.

> **Brainstorming or 'blame storming'?**
> One of our favourite stories about brainstorming comes from a customer who described the brainstorming process within their organization as really 'blame storming'. Their senior leadership got together to analyse the problem with the primary focus being about defending their territory and attempting to lay blame on another department. Given the understanding that 'blame storming' may be a common challenge in the problem management process, we often find it helpful to only include in the brainstorming session people who are actually working to solve the problem. This builds teamwork and keeps the focus on root cause analysis. While this may not be an issue for more mature IT organizations, for organizations that are just getting started with problem management and root cause analysis, this is good advice.

The brainstorming discussion is usually facilitated by the problem manager using one or more techniques. The technique we recommend is to use sticky notes (or some form of digital data capture) as a way of gathering ideas about possible causes and solutions. The facilitator will hand out sticky notes to each individual in the room, asking them to write down possible causes of the problem, each on a separate sticky note. No discussion occurs at this point. The facilitator then gathers all of the sticky notes and puts them up on a whiteboard or wall. He/she points to the first one and asks, 'Whose idea is this?' That person is then allowed to explain why they thought this was the cause of the problem.

Attendees may ask questions at this point, for clarification. However, the facilitator needs to ensure that no judging or criticism occurs. Once all of the proposed causes have been explained and discussed, a vote is taken where the attendees are asked to select their top two or three choices that they feel are most likely the cause.

> **Note**
> It is a good idea to have attendees vote by ballot to eliminate the potential for peer pressure.

Those causes with the most votes are then brought forward for discussion regarding possible solutions. The same process is used for gathering ideas regarding possible solutions. Sticky notes are handed out to each individual in the room asking them to write down possible solutions to the causes that received the most votes. The sticky notes are gathered, discussed and voted on. The last step in the technique is to document, agree and assign actions to prove the chosen solutions.

Let's see what the output of this technique might look like. Take the following scenario:

'FIN001' server crashed at 3.00 a.m. on 8 August, affecting all users of the FINANCIAL application at all business locations, after the on-call Windows engineer applied a vendor patch to the server residing in rack 23 within the Scottsdale data centre.

We will assume that we have completed our brainstorming session to identify possible causes and solutions. The output from this brainstorming session might look similar to the contents of Table 3.5.

Brainstorming is a fairly simple and straightforward technique. The benefits of using the technique as we have described above are that it is useful for generating a lot of ideas, it is

Table 3.5 Example output from a brainstorming RCA technique

Possible causes	Possible solutions
Patch was bad	Back out patch and contact vendor
Wrong patch was applied	Validate patch number and that prerequisites have been applied
Patch triggered another problem	Research and apply additional patches
Procedure for applying patch was not followed	Provide training; provide discipline/corrective action; implement quality control measures
Procedure for applying patch was in error	Re-create and test the procedure on a test server
Patch was applied from wrong source	Apply patch from correct source
Lost power to the server	Implement redundant power or UPS

easy, it reduces domination by individuals with strong personalities and it facilitates consensus-driven prioritization of ideas. The downside to this technique is that it may appear to be too mechanical in its execution and often does not examine all available data.

3.2.5.3 Chronological analysis

This technique establishes a timeline, or diary of all the events/activities that took place leading up to the problem as well as all the activities that have taken place to the present time.

> **The importance of chronological analysis**
> As IT organizations become more mature, they are frequently able to establish an event timeline from system monitoring tools, and an activity timeline from ITSM tools. However, many IT organizations have events occurring and activities taking place that are not being formally captured. Regardless of whether the data is being captured by tools or if this timeline is built retroactively from interviewing staff, chronological analysis is an important root cause analysis technique. By pulling together the correct investigation and diagnosis team and performing analysis on the chronological timeline of events, you will frequently discover that information related to the problem has not been shared across the functional support groups, and in some cases work is being done and changes are being made that have not been shared (or analysed) across the teams. By determining which events triggered other events, or which activities triggered other activities, correlation and causality may quickly help to identify the root cause.

Chronological analysis involves five steps:

- Develop a timeline documenting all events in chronological order
- Determine which events triggered other events
- Discount claims that are not supported by evidence (eliminate 'noise')
- Correlate and identify root cause
- Attempt to re-create the problem, if practical, to confirm root cause.

Let's see what this might look like in practice by looking at a scenario involving an imaginary company:

Betterbake staff from multiple locations are unable to use the BAKER application and this is preventing them from accessing online cake recipes.

An investigation and diagnosis team consisting of several representatives from technical support groups was formed to determine the root cause using the chronological analysis RCA technique. During the meeting, the facilitator used a blank template (with the column headings reflected in Table 3.6) to capture the events surrounding the problem. These events were then sorted by date and time. This sorted sequence of events became the chronological timeline.

After further review and discussion of the events as they occurred, the investigation and diagnosis team determined the following potential causes and likely root cause:

Table 3.6 Example of sorted events surrounding the scenario problem

Date	Time	Location(s) affected	Reported by	Event occurrence	Support personnel involved	Action taken by support personnel	Potential number of users affected	Affected or suspected CI
7 Aug. 2010	4.15 am	Scottsdale		Database reorganized	Database administrator	Purged old records and reorganized database	All users of the BAKER application	BAKR-DB1 (supports the BAKER application)
8 Aug. 2010	1.30 am	Scottsdale		Patch was applied to server BAKR001	Windows engineer	Patch applied and server rebooted	All users of the BAKER application	BAKR001 (supports the BAKER application)
8 Aug. 2010	2.32 am	Scottsdale	Computer operator	Data centre lost power	Data centre manager	Contacted city engineer	All	Trunk line (power into the data centre)
8 Aug. 2010	2.54 am	Scottsdale	City engineer	Trunk line was restored	Data centre manager	Updated the service desk	All	Trunk line (power into the data centre)
8 Aug. 2010	3.01 am	Scottsdale	Jane Smith, chocolate cake baker	Stated she can't get into BAKER application	Service desk	Asked her to reboot her PC	Only her	BAKER application
8 Aug. 2010	3.16 am	Scottsdale	Jane Smith, chocolate cake baker	Stated the reboot did not fix her issue	Service desk	Transferred ticket to application support group	Only her	BAKER application
8 Aug. 2010	3.52 am	Multiple	Multiple bakers calling into service desk	Bakers stating they can't get into BAKER application	Bob Doe, BAKER application support group	Transferred ticket to server support group	Multiple bakers, multiple locations unable to access application	BAKR001 server; the application is running fine on redundant server BAKR002

- **Potential causes** Database reorganization; power outage; network problem; patch applied.
- **Likely root cause** Patch applied to the BAKR001 server caused the unavailability of the BAKER application.

Reorganizing the BAKR-DB1 database was a potential cause, but they eliminated it as the root cause since the application had been running for nearly 24 hours after the reorganization with no reported problems. They also eliminated the loss of the trunk line that supplies power into the data centre as the root cause since the only known CI that was being affected was the BAKER application. If power were the cause, they would have expected to see an impact on several other CIs within the infrastructure, not just the BAKER application. The network could have been the cause, but they would have expected other applications and software, including email, to not be accessible. However, there was no indication that this was the case. Thus, they were left with the conclusion that the patch applied to BAKR001 caused the failure. They would need to do further testing to determine if the patch itself was bad, or if the procedure for applying the patch was not followed.

We suggest combining this technique with other techniques for any RCA efforts. Chronological analysis is especially useful for complex problems with conflicting reports about what happened.

> **Note**
> Successful use of this technique involves capturing information that is relevant to the problem, performing analysis of that information and eliminating those events that are merely 'noise'.

3.2.5.4 Ishikawa diagrams ('fishbone' diagrams)

Kaoru Ishikawa was a Japanese quality management process pioneer in the 1960s. His diagrams are often referred to as 'fishbone' diagrams because of their shape. You may also hear them referred to as 'cause and effect' diagrams. The diagrams help with identification of all possible causes and effects of a problem, or where something may be improved. This technique brings a more formal and structured approach to brainstorming and works well with cross-functional teams. However, it can be challenging to identify the root cause out of all the possible causes identified.

> **Tip**
> Ishikawa diagrams are particularly helpful during the brainstorming process to keep the RCA team mindful of various broad categories (ribs) that might have otherwise been overlooked. The downside to using these diagrams is that the brainstorming process may be slowed down as the team debates which broad category the potential cause would best fit into.

Problem management activities

The Ishikawa diagram technique involves the following steps:

- Define the problem (spine and head of the fish, i.e. the effect)
- List broad categories of the possible main causes (ribs)
- Use brainstorming techniques to get participants to suggest possible causes
- Note possible causes on the appropriate main cause branch (rib) of the diagram
- Rank the top causes based on experience and available data
- Identify possible solutions to the most likely cause.

Figure 3.4 shows what an Ishikawa diagram might look like for mapping the causes of the following problem scenario:

Recently, Betterbake has seen an increase in returned cakes across multiple store locations. Each returned cake order is logged as an incident and the cake(s) are quickly replaced. Headquarters wants to know why these cakes are being returned.

In our example, the broad categories of possible causes (ribs) were technology, people, environment and process. Several variations of these broad categories are in use by companies in various industries. Manufacturing companies often use what is referred to as the 4Ms – machines, methods, materials and manpower, while a marketing organization might use people, product, process and procedure. There is no 'one-size-fits-all' set of categories. When in doubt, use the four classifications of root causes we listed earlier in this chapter – physical, system, human and organizational.

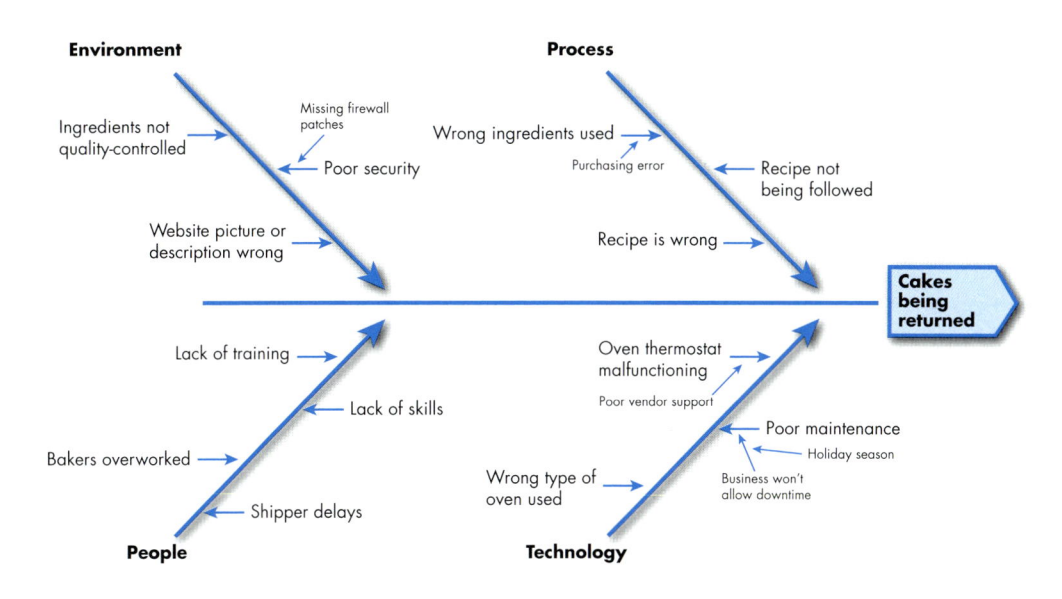

Figure 3.4 Example of an Ishikawa diagram

In some cases a possible cause can have additional lower-level causes which are listed as sub-branches on the diagram. Once the diagram has been fully fleshed out, the top potential causes are ranked based on experience and available data (this can be done using the brainstorming technique discussed earlier). Then, possible solutions to the most likely cause are discussed and agreed to and action is taken to prove the solution.

3.2.5.5 Pareto analysis

This technique is used to identify the most important potential causes, based on frequency of occurrence. It is named after Vilfredo Pareto, an Italian engineer and economist, and is often referred to as the Pareto principle, the 'law of the vital few', or the '80/20 rule' – roughly 80% of the events come from 20% of the causes. This technique presumes that cause-related data is available for analysis. While less useful for the identification of root cause, this technique helps to identify where to spend time and resources on improving a situation or fixing a problem.

Pareto analysis employs the following steps:

- Develop a table with the first column listing causes and the second column indicating frequency of occurrence for each cause
- Arrange the causes based on frequency of occurrence (most frequently occurring cause first)
- Add a cumulative percentage column to the table
- Use this table to create a histogram of the causes (bars are arranged in order of their percentage of the total count)
- Identify the top causes which have a cumulative total of approximately 80%
- Focus initially on these as the primary causes for improving the situation or fixing the problem.

Let's see what this looks like in practice given the following scenario:

There has been an increase in dissatisfaction with the service desk according to customer satisfaction surveys. We need to determine the cause and take appropriate action.

Based on the surveys that were returned, the data is organized in tabular form as shown in Table 3.7.

The first two columns list possible causes and their total number of occurrences (i.e. the number of times that particular cause was stated as the reason for being dissatisfied with the service desk). The next column reflects the '% of total' (i.e. their frequency as a percentage of the total cause count). The final column reflects the 'Cumulative %'.

Problem management activities

Table 3.7 Pareto analysis of customer dissatisfaction with service desk

Causes	Total number by cause	Percentage of total	Cumulative percentage
Too long on hold	60	50%	50%
Staff not courteous	35	29%	79%
Staff not knowledgeable	10	8%	87%
Transferred too many times	6	5%	92%
Hard to understand	4	3%	95%
Poor communication	2	2%	97%
No follow-up	2	2%	98%
No out-of-hours staffing	2	2%	100%
	121		

We can see that being on hold too long was the cause of dissatisfaction on 60 surveys, accounting for 50% of the dissatisfied customers. The next most frequent cause was that staff were not courteous. This cause was reported 35 times and reflects 29% of the total reports. Adding the % total from each row (top to bottom) gives us the cumulative percentage column.

Those causes that cumulatively represent approximately 80% of the dissatisfaction should be our areas for focus. In this case, 'Too long on hold' and 'Staff not courteous' represent approximately 80% of the dissatisfaction. We should focus our attention on finding solutions for these two causes.

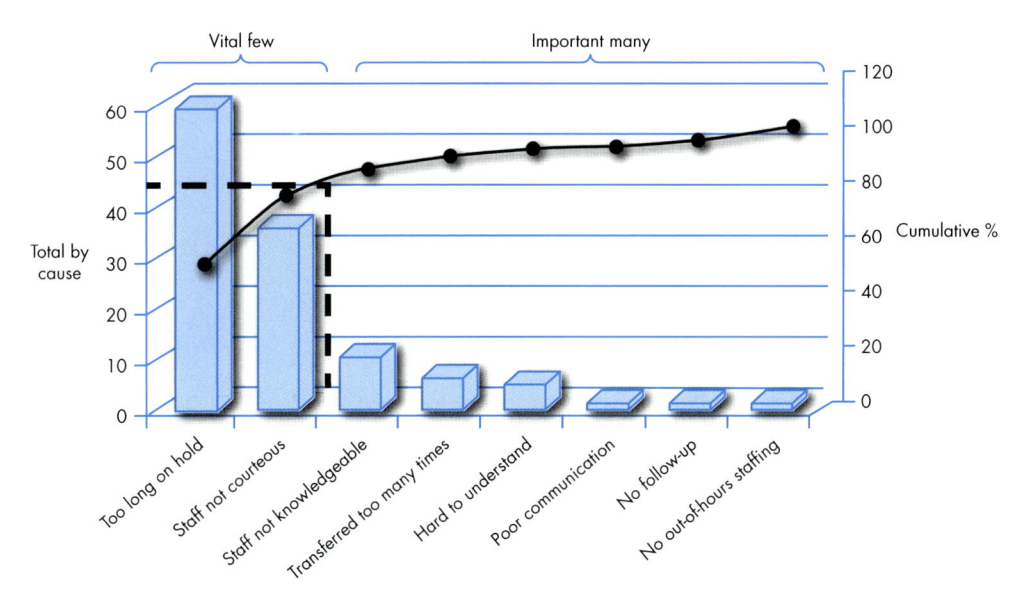

Figure 3.5 Pareto chart of causes for customer dissatisfaction

We can represent this data visually in the form of a histogram, as shown in Figure 3.5. Across the bottom are the causes of customer dissatisfaction. The left axis reflects counts for each cause. The right axis reflects percentages of the total count. The black line reflects the cumulative percentage. The dashed line shows those causes that represent approximately 80% of the total of all causes. These are the two causes that the organization will want to focus its attention on and develop permanent fixes for.

In summary, the Pareto chart highlights the most important causes, or sources of defects, among a set of causes. This approach is statistical in nature, and therefore it leaves a positive perception with stakeholders that the service provider has done its homework. However, the technique is only as accurate as the available data.

3.2.5.6 Kepner–Tregoe

This is a structured methodology for rational decision-making through the gathering, prioritization and evaluation of information. It was developed by Dr Charles Kepner and Dr Benjamin Tregoe in the 1960s. There are four basic steps when using the Kepner–Tregoe decision matrix. They are situation appraisal (clarify and prioritize the situation), problem analysis (find the root cause), decision analysis (select the best fix) and potential problem analysis (avoid future problems). Numerous multi-day courses are available providing in-depth training on the Kepner–Tregoe technique.

We have limited our focus to the problem analysis component of this technique (getting to the root cause). There are five steps to Kepner–Tregoe problem analysis:

- Define the problem
- Describe the problem in terms of:
    - Identity – What does not function well?
    - Location – Where does this occur?
    - Time – When did this occur (or frequency)?
    - Size – What is the extent of the problem; how many are affected?
- Establish possible causes
- Test the probable causes
- Verify the true cause.

Let's see what this looks like in practice given the following scenario.

Problem management activities

> **Scenario**
> A healthcare organization uses an electronic medical record (EMR) database for storing patient information. This 'database' actually consists of two databases: EMR-DB1 holds records for patients whose last name begins with the letters A–M and EMR-DB2 holds records for patients whose last name begins with the letters N–Z.
>
> The EMR-DB1 database was quickly reaching its maximum storage capacity. A decision was made to reorganize it on 14 May at 5.00 a.m. after a program ran to archive patient records which had no activity during the past 12 months. Archiving these patient records and reorganizing the database would significantly reduce EMR-DB1's storage use.
>
> That same morning, a new program was put into production that runs nightly against both EMR databases (EMR-DB1 and EMR-DB2) and automatically archives patient records with no activity from today's date, minus 12 months. This will effectively prevent both databases from reaching maximum storage capacity for some time.
>
> Since 14 May there have been several calls to the service desk reporting an increasing number of missing patient records that should be present in the EMR-DB1 database.

Define the problem

By asking some basic questions we can more accurately define the problem and possible causes. One method for this is to ask the 5 Ws.

- **Who is experiencing the problem?** Users of the EMR system.
- **What are the effects or symptoms?** Some patient records are missing from the EMR-DB1 database.
- **Where does the problem occur?** At all hospitals and clinics using the EMR system.
- **When does the problem occur or when did it start happening?** The problem was first reported on 14 May.
- **Why is this significant?** The number of instances or calls to the service desk is increasing.

Describe the problem

In this step we will describe four aspects of any problem: what does not function well, where does this problem occur, when and/or how frequently does this problem occur, and what is the extent of the problem (how many are affected). The work we completed in Step 1 will help us answer several of these questions.

We will begin by describing what the problem 'is' (similar to what we did in Step 1), and then we will go on to describe what the problem 'could be but is not'. This approach will help us to describe the problem in even more detail, and it will help us focus on possible causes.

Table 3.8 has been filled out based on our scenario.

In the case of existing systems that have been working properly up to some point in time without incident, we should consider looking at recent changes that have been made. By

Table 3.8 'Could be' but 'is not' table

	Is	Could be but is not	Differences
What	EMR-DB1	EMR-DB2	EMR-DB2 records were not archived and database was not reorganized
Where	In production	Test lab	Archive program ran from different execution libraries
When	After 14 May	Before 14 May	Archive program ran; database reorganized; nightly archive program implemented on 14 May
Extent	EMR-DB1: 40+ instances	EMR-DB2: Stable	Number of instances increasing daily

looking at what the problem is and is not, we are able to establish what changes could have had an impact, and those that would not have. When listing changes in the 'Differences' column, we are concerned about those changes which may have had an impact on the 'Is' column. Note that sometimes underlying problems may have existed for some time and were just exposed by a recent change.

- **What?** We know that EMR-DB1 is having the problem and not EMR-DB2. What is the difference/change? The only significant difference is that EMR-DB2 records were not archived and the database was not reorganized. That may be an indication of the root cause.

- **Where?** We know that the problem occurred in production, but it did not occur in the test lab. What is the difference/change? The difference is that the archive program ran from two different execution libraries. This may or may not be relevant.

- **When?** When did the problem occur? It occurred after 14 May, but it did not occur at any prior time. What is the difference/change? The archive program ran, the database was reorganized and a new program was put into production. These differences may lead us to a significant conclusion.

- **Extent** It occurred on only one of the two databases and we have had multiple calls about it. What is the difference/change? The other database appears to be stable, while the number of calls on EMR-DB1 is increasing.

Establish possible causes

The differences and changes from the 'is/is not' table become potential causes of why the problem occurred and one of them might be the root cause. We now build our 'true if' table to start identifying potential causes for testing.

Problem management activities

Table 3.9 'True if' table

Potential causes	True if	Probable root cause?
Records were lost during the EMR-DB1 database reorganization	Missing records are only from EMR-DB1 Final EMR-DB1 record count from the initial archive program does not match the final record count from the reorganization job	Perhaps
Nightly archive program in error	Missing records had activity within the last 12 months Missing records are from both EMR databases	Probably not
EMR-DB1 initial archive program in error	Missing records had activity within the last 12 months Nightly archive program is correctly archiving patient records	Probably

Table 3.9 is the 'true if' table which has been completed to show what this would look like for our scenario.

The potential cause in the first column might be the root cause if the statements about the cause in the second column are true.

Test the probable causes

We now need to determine the likelihood that each of these potential causes is the root cause. For each possible cause ask if this is the root cause of this problem. Does it explain everything the problem is and what the problem could be but is not?'

- **For the first potential cause** It is true that missing records are only from EMR-DB1. But we would need to check the record count at the end of the run from the initial archive program against the record count coming out of the run of the database reorganization. If they are the same, then this is likely not to be the root cause.

- **For the second potential cause** It is true we have missing records that had activity within the last 12 months. This is evidenced by the number of phone calls to the service desk. But, we need to check if we had missing records coming from both EMR databases. So far, this has not been reported and therefore this is likely not the root cause.

- **For the third potential cause** We do have missing records that had activity within the last 12 months, **and** the applications support group confirmed the nightly archive program is correctly archiving patient records on a going-forward basis. Thus, the initial archive program was likely in error (due perhaps to a faulty starting archive date) and is therefore the likely root cause.

Verify the true cause

The final step is to test your conclusion. Here we compare the probable cause against the problem description to determine if it satisfies all of the conditions (true if) of the problem. Once we've identified a probable cause that explains all of the conditions it must be tested. This is done by reproducing the same conditions to see if it results in the same symptoms. If it does, we have confirmed the cause.

Once we are confident that we have identified the root cause of the problem, a solution must be developed and implemented following the change and release management processes. After the solution has been implemented it needs to be tested under the same conditions to ensure the issue does not recur.

Summary thoughts on Kepner–Tregoe

We want to reiterate that this is one of the more involved and complex RCA techniques. While it can be a time-consuming method to determine root cause, it is a mature, well-documented and detailed technique. It is especially useful when there are many potential causes.

3.2.5.7 Fault tree analysis

This is a top-down diagnostic tool used to identify links between possible causes.

This technique uses Boolean logic to show the relationship of lower-level causes and their effect on higher-level causes that led to the problem or failure.

The top event (top of the tree) is the problem. All the events that could cause the top event are listed beneath the top event and connected by logic expressions (Boolean operators). Each of these events (possible causes) could have one or many sub-events (lower-level causes) connected via logic expressions.

Here are the steps involved in this technique:

- List the problem at the top of the tree
- Brainstorm possible causes
- Determine if there are lower-level causes
- Use Boolean logic gates to indicate relationships.

Let's use the following scenario to demonstrate this technique:

'BAKR001' server crashed unexpectedly at 9.30 a.m. on 10 August affecting all users of the BAKER application at the Scottsdale Mall store location.

Figure 3.6 represents one possible fault tree analysis diagram for this problem.

For our scenario, the problem was a server outage. Next, three possible causes were identified, each were then fleshed out with multiple lower-level causes. Let's see what the diagram is showing us.

Problem management activities

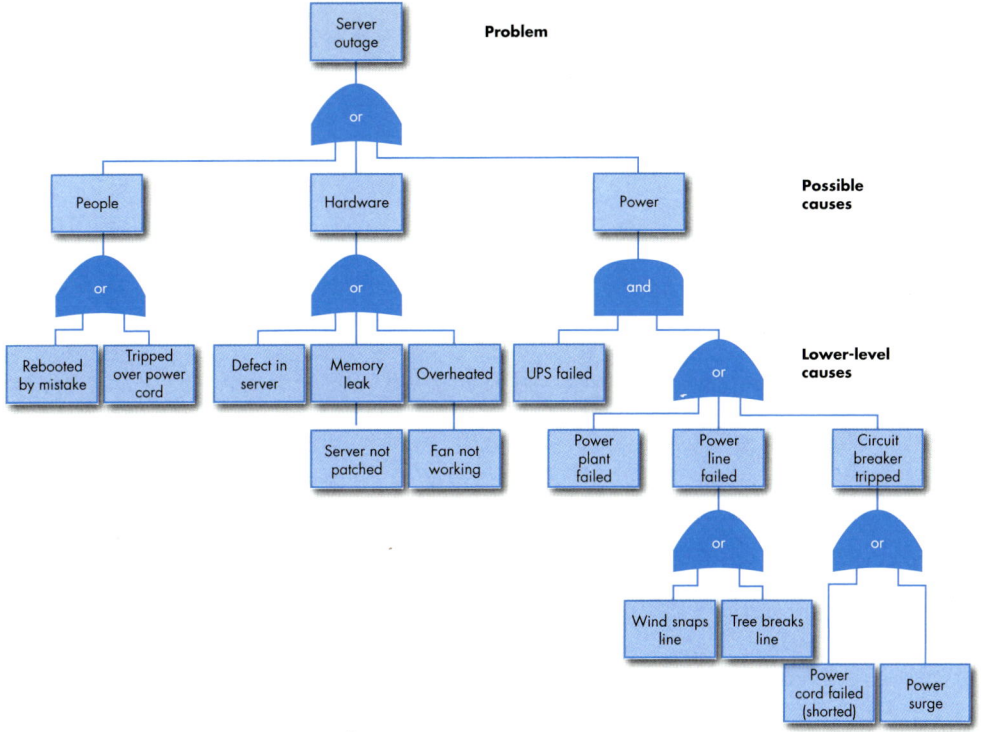

Figure 3.6 Fault tree analysis diagram

The server outage could have been caused by:

- People, or
- Hardware, or
- Power failure.

If the outage was caused by people, it would have been caused by:

- Rebooting the server by mistake, or
- Someone tripped over the power cord.

If the outage was caused by hardware, it would have been caused by:

- A defect in the server, or
- A memory leak, or
- The server overheated.

If a memory leak caused the hardware to fail, it would have been caused by:

- The server not being patched.

65

If the server overheated, it would have been caused by:

- The fan not working.

If the outage was caused by a power failure, it would have been caused by:

- The UPS failing and one of these other conditions:
    - The power plant had a failure, or
    - The power line failed, or
    - The circuit breaker tripped.

If the power line failed, it would have been caused by:

- The wind snapping the line, or
- A tree falling and breaking the line.

If the circuit breaker tripped, it would have been caused by:

- A short in the power cord, or
- A power surge.

Using this technique enables you to identify the links between possible causes, and ultimately leads you to the root cause. It is useful for identifying causal relationships and whether these causal relationships are related to the root cause.

3.2.6 Which root cause analysis technique should I use?

First of all, you are not limited to using just one technique. Combining various RCA techniques is often a useful practice. As an example, brainstorming and chronological analysis are often used in combination with several of the other RCA techniques. Over time, organizations will figure out which RCA techniques are most useful for a particular type of problem, as well as which techniques are best suited for use by a particular functional team. Here are some parting suggestions regarding RCA:

- Start your analysis with a timeline of events (chronological analysis)
- Use brainstorming to identify all possible causes and solutions
- Post your work for others to see/use – this will help to institutionalize RCA practices within your organization.

3.3 Resolution and recovery

There are two activities associated with problem resolution: solution identification and solution implementation.

3.3.1 Solution identification

Solution identification involves identification of CIs which should be repaired, replaced or removed from the infrastructure. There are a couple of points to recall:

- We often think that the problem management process is all about finding the root cause, but that is only a means to the end. After identifying the root cause, the real goal of problem management is the permanent fix.
- Don't just fix the symptoms or problem, fix the root cause.

After identifying the true root cause, research and discussion needs to occur regarding what might fix this problem or known error permanently. As with determining root cause, identifying a permanent fix may be an individual effort, or it may involve a team, or a cross-functional team. In some cases suppliers and service partners may also need to be involved in the identification of the solution. Keep in mind that there may be multiple solutions to a problem, or that a solution may involve multiple actions or tasks. As an example, the solution may include implementing a new maintenance schedule, updating current policies, and training specific users or IT staff.

Each possible solution needs to be evaluated and a determination made by the individual or the team regarding which solution to pursue. Identifying the steps to prevent this problem from happening again also needs to occur. You may have had a problem with a particular server and have identified a permanent fix for it. However, there may be multiple servers of that same make and model that have the potential for that same problem and they will also need to be fixed.

Once a solution is identified and agreed to, we have reached another process control point where permission to proceed with the development of the proposed solution must be obtained. This may simply be a matter of gaining approval from the problem manager or an IT manager. In other cases financial justification might be necessary and a formal business case should be developed when the solution will be costly, complex, time-consuming or involve more resources.

> **Note**
> In some cases, the business may decide to leave the known error open and continue to use the workaround due to the cost or risk of developing and/or implementing the change, or due to the insignificance of the service impact to the affected business areas.

Factors to consider when determining whether to proceed with the proposed solution include:

- The effort required to maintain the workaround or temporary solution
- The impact on productivity of the customers and support staff
- The cost of service interruption and/or the cost of penalties from a degraded service

- The cost of the permanent solution
- The impact on customer satisfaction
- Service level commitments.

When approval to develop the proposed solution has been obtained, the solution should be developed and tested to confirm the proposed solution does indeed fix the problem or known error. This may involve multiple technical support groups and should be coordinated by release management. It is important that proper testing should occur on the proposed solution to ensure that we solve problems and not introduce new ones into the environment through the changing of CIs.

3.3.2 Solution implementation

Once the solution has been developed and tested, problem management works with change and release management to develop an implementation plan. Solution implementation involves actions taken to approve, implement and validate the proposed solution to the problem or known error.

It is important that changes to CIs be approved by change management and the problem or known error record linked to the change record, thus establishing a relationship between incident management, problem management, change management, release management and configuration management. This information is important for trending, RCA and reporting. If there is an urgency to implement the fix, the change should be expedited through the change management process.

Once implementation approval has been obtained, problem management will work with change and release management to execute the implementation plan. When the permanent fix has been implemented, change and problem management should work together to verify that the solution corrected the error. For some solutions, this may take some time. For example, if the problem was related to a monthly or quarterly report, it may take two or three cycles before the solution can be confirmed. Meanwhile, the problem or known error record status should indicate that it is still open, pending verification. Subsequent to solution implementation, problem prevention activities or post-implementation tasks should be executed.

3.3.3 Setting process targets

While setting goals and objectives for the time to resolve a problem is a worthy and necessary consideration, for organizations just getting started with problem management we suggest not setting target resolution times for problems. There are a couple of reasons for this. First, you likely have no history or knowledge of how long it takes to resolve different categories of problems. So setting target resolution times for problems would, for the most part, be guesswork. Secondly, problem resolution may be less urgent because

Problem management activities

you have workarounds in place to restore the service. As your problem management process becomes more mature, then consider setting target resolution times for problems by category and/or technology domain.

Setting a time target for the identification of the root cause should be considered even at the earliest stages of process maturity. This target is more achievable for less mature organizations and it is important that activities supporting RCA occur as quickly as possible after the problem has been identified.

> **Crime scene investigation**
> What is one of the first things the police do when a crime has been committed, especially a serious crime? They quickly cordon off the area to preserve any evidence and prevent contamination of the crime scene. Then they go in and start their examination and investigation while all of the clues and the evidence are fresh. This should be true for problem management as well. You want to preserve activity logs and journals, voicemails and emails, and conduct interviews with individuals who have experienced the problem while all of the data and information is present and memories are fresh. This information will be critical for quickly getting to the root cause.

Table 3.10 provides an example of how an organization might set time targets for getting to the root cause of problems. The problem priority levels in Table 3.10 are the same as the incident priority levels shown in Table 2.7, although the time parameters are different.

Table 3.10 Setting time parameters for problems

Problem priority	Time parameters (from the opening of a problem record)
Priority 1	The root cause should be identified, documented and communicated within 24 hours
	The problem record must be updated every 4 hours with status information until the root cause has been found, with communications occurring at the same interval to the service desk
	The problem record cannot be placed in a pending status unless awaiting action from a supplier or service provider partner
Priority 2	The root cause should be identified, documented and communicated within 5 business days
	The problem record must be updated with status information daily
	The problem record cannot be placed in a pending status unless awaiting action from a supplier or service provider partner
Priority 3	The root cause should be identified, documented and communicated within 30 business days
	The problem record must be updated with status information weekly
Priority 4	The root cause should be identified, documented and communicated within 60 business days
	The problem record must be updated with status information monthly

If a technical support group member is assigned multiple problem records with the same priority and similar deadlines, how would they know which one to work on first? This is where linking incidents to problems and looking at the number of incidents linked to a problem record is beneficial. For example, if the first priority 2 record has two incidents linked to it and the second priority 2 record has seven incidents linked to it, then you should probably work on the second record because it is probably having a greater impact upon the business than the first. If all other elements are equal (priority and deadline), consider the relative impacts of the two records as the tiebreaker for which to work on first.

3.4 Closure

Once the solution has been confirmed as having fixed the problem or known error (there are no new incidents related to the problem), the status of the problem or known error record should then be marked as resolved. The assignee should update the knowledge base or known error database with resolution information, clearly outlining the tasks and scope of the corrective actions. Documentation should be clear, detailed, accurate and timely so that the information is accessible and searchable in the unlikely event the incident or problem should resurface in the future. Instructions and formats on how to enter the information should be provided, including the usage of searchable key words. Ideally, the ITSM tool should enforce data entry standardization to improve completeness and accuracy of the information. Most ITSM tools allow you to record the resolution and root cause via the use of codes. Examples of resolution and root cause codes can be found in Appendix D. The purpose and benefits of recording this information are to:

- Expedite the resolution of future incidents and problems
- Improve consistency in the application of the solution
- Reduce duplication of resolution efforts
- Reduce the cost of service support
- Improve reporting and trending analysis.

As the final control point within the problem management process, the problem manager or problem queue manager should verify the problem (or known error) record is complete and accurate. If it is, they should mark the record as closed. When appropriate, and based upon organizational criteria that have been established for when a post-implementation review should occur, conduct such a review for capturing lessons learned to be applied to future problems. Criteria for which problems to review might include: sensitive technology domains; priority 1 and 2 problems that missed their target resolution times; major problems; and problems related to new services that are less than six months old.

Once the problem or known error record has been closed, any related open incidents should be closed. Figure 3.7 shows the relationship and normal process flow between process records, from the opening of an incident to its permanent fix.

Problem management activities

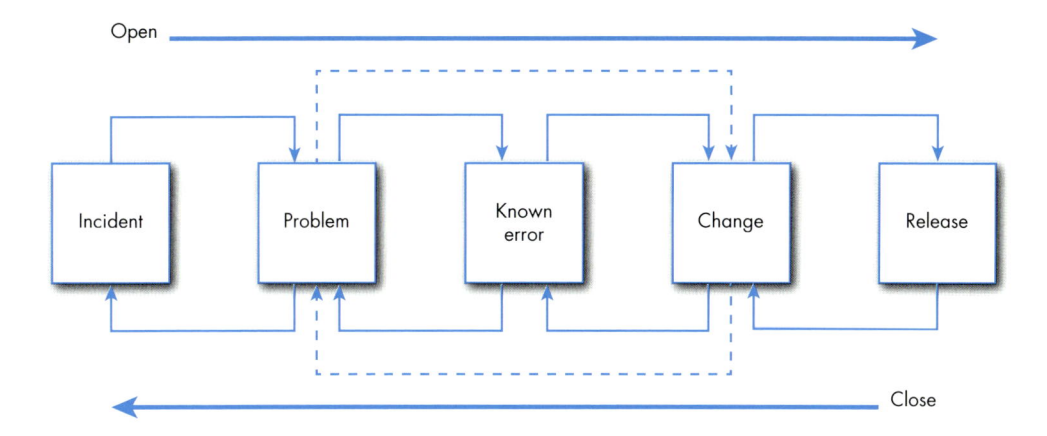

Figure 3.7 Process record relationships

Figure 3.7 can be explained as follows:

- An incident occurs and an incident record is opened.
- Based upon organizational criteria a problem record is opened.
- If the root cause and a workaround are identified, a known error record is created.

    Keep in mind that a problem is referred to as a known error only when there is an identified root cause and a workaround. You might have identified the root cause but have no workaround, or you might have identified a workaround but you do not know what the root cause is. Unless both are identified, it remains a problem. Note that some ITSM tools do not have separate records for a problem and a known error. Instead, when a problem has a root cause and workaround identified it is simply a status change to the problem record, denoting that it is now a known error.

- Once a permanent solution is identified and documented, a change record is created to seek approval for implementing the permanent solution. The submission of the request for change to change management may be triggered by the problem record (represented by the dotted arrow) or by the known error record (solid arrow).
- The permanent solution may be a simple change, or it may be built, tested and implemented through the disciplines of release management.
- Once the solution is confirmed as working and no more incidents are occurring, the release record is closed, the related change record is closed, the known error record related to the change is closed, the problem record related to the known error is closed and any associated open incidents are closed.

We sometimes are asked if a problem record should ever be closed as 'unresolved'. Our answer to that question is 'yes'. There could be a number of reasons why an organization decides to close a problem record as unresolved:

71

- The problem was unique, occurred once and is not reproducible
- The problem has a low business impact
- The solution is too costly to implement
- The business is willing to live with the workaround.

Clear criteria should be established and agreed as to when a problem record can be closed as unresolved. This decision comes about as a result of a discussion between the problem assignee, the problem manager and a customer representative.

A related question is whether problems that were closed as 'unresolved' should ever be revisited. After all, you may now have a permanent solution to fix the problem, or you may have identified a better workaround. There is no single right answer as to when, if ever, to revisit those problems. It really comes down to an organizational decision. Our advice would be to use the following criteria to determine if/when to review records in this status and take action on them:

- Incidents continue to occur (perhaps no workaround is available)
- The workaround is not very effective (is not simple, or quick and easy to apply)
- The cost or effort of the permanent solution has gone down
- Some external factor changes the equation of cost/risk/impact to the point where the workaround needs to get replaced with a permanent solution.

3.4.1 Service disruption report

As previously discussed, incidents and problems will vary in impact and can result in a service disruption to one or more users. When the service disruption has been significant, there may be times when it is appropriate to send out a communication to the affected users and other stakeholders providing them with information about what, when, why and how the service disruption occurred, along with what was done to fix and prevent it from happening again. This information is often documented in what is referred to as an 'incident report' or 'service disruption report'. Problem management is an important contributor to the writing of this report.

The purpose of the service disruption report is to:

- Serve as a communication tool to users and stakeholders
- Build and maintain confidence and trust in the service provider
- Document details of the incident or problem, its impact and the steps taken to resolve it
- Indicate the actionable steps that have been or will be taken to prevent recurrence.

The report should be sent out after service is restored and, ideally, after the root cause has been identified. It should be precise, honest, empathetic, serious and reflect a positive tone. Finger pointing should never occur. In fact, we recommend you seldom, if ever, use names. The report should not contain empty promises such as 'We will do everything we can to ensure this never happens again'. It should state clearly what went wrong, the steps taken to restore service and what you're doing to prevent it from happening again, by when. It should look and sound professional with well-constructed, grammatically correct sentences in 'customer-speak', not 'tech-speak'. The use of abbreviations and acronyms should be limited and they should always be defined.

When writing the report, consider how and what you're saying from the following three perspectives:

- **Confidentiality** What can and cannot be included
- **Liability** Be careful not to place your organization at risk
- **Competition** Service providers with external customers must be careful not to include information that would make you vulnerable to competition.

Common content in the report usually consists of the following:

- Title
- Start/end date and time of the service outage
- Customer(s) affected (estimate, if necessary)
- Outage summary
    - Short description, its duration, impact and root cause (if known)
- Outage details
    - Sequence of events that occurred and actions taken
- Business impact
    - Business processes impacted
    - Locations affected
- Root cause (provide details)
- Preventive actions
    - Itemized list of actions to prevent it from happening again (with target completion dates).

An example of a 'service disruption report' is provided in Appendix F.

3.5 Major problem review

A major problem is any problem where the impact to the organization was significant enough that management decides to review activities associated with the investigation, diagnosis and resolution of the problem. In essence, the actions and interactions of people, process and technology are reviewed and assessed.

A major problem sounds like a major incident but we said that an incident never becomes a problem, so is a major incident synonymous with a major problem? No, although they may both be occurring simultaneously. Let's use an example.

A virus outbreak may be classified as a major incident as it is likely having or will have a significant productivity impact on the organization. Incident management is focused on restoring the service as quickly as possible – getting users back up and running and recovered from the effects of the virus. We also need problem management to identify containment measures and get to the root cause so that we can prevent this from spreading further and from ever happening again. Provided there are sufficient available resources, major incident and major problem processes may be operating simultaneously.

Within days of the major problem being resolved, a major problem review should occur. The review meeting will usually be led by the problem manager. Alternatively, the meeting could be led by a neutral but experienced facilitator who was not involved in the problem but who knows the processes, systems, tools and staff involved in the problem. Preparation, data collection and participation should follow the guidelines provided earlier, in the section on forming an investigation and diagnosis team (section 3.2.3).

The purpose of this meeting should be to review process, actions and tools to discover:

- What went well?
    - Identify what went according to plan
    - Identify actions, techniques or procedures that others can use in the future
- What didn't go well?
    - Identify the issues and actions that were not helpful or were ineffective so they can be eliminated in future situations
- What can be done better in the future?
    - Identify actions that are focused on improvements, not failures
- How can we prevent recurrence?
    - Identify and assign actions that should prevent this from happening again
- How did suppliers and service partners perform?
    - Identify and assign follow-up actions.

The meeting should have a positive and collaborative atmosphere where all comments are welcome and participation is encouraged. The goal is to learn and improve from actions taken or not taken. Note that when discussing the people aspect of the problem, caution should be taken not to point fingers, lay blame, or find fault.

The meeting discussions should be documented and a report should be prepared and distributed immediately following the meeting to participants, management, customers, suppliers and other support groups. The report should include information such as:

- Names of team participants
- Data collected and discussed at the meeting
- Timeline of events (chronological analysis)
- Systems, tools and personnel involved in the problem and its resolution
- Actions, techniques and procedures that were effective and those that were ineffective
- Open action items and assigned responsibilities.

4 Problem management relationships

The problem management process interfaces with several other ITSM processes and its activities are performed by several IT functions or functional teams. In this chapter, we will look at those processes and functions which have the closest relationships to problem management. These processes or functions provide information, receive information or perform an action that enables problem management to determine the root cause, or create and implement solutions for service restoration. For each of these processes and functions, we will provide a brief description and then in tables (Tables 4.1 to 4.9) list their inputs to, and outputs from, problem management.

4.1 Problem management's relationships to other ITSM processes

4.1.1 Service level management

Service level management (SLM) defines and manages service levels for the services the IT service provider delivers to its customers. These service levels are described in service level agreements (SLAs). As a reminder, an SLA is a documented and signed agreement between the IT service provider and one or more customers describing the IT services that will be provided, service level targets for delivering those services, hours of service availability and support, service pricing and specific responsibilities of both parties.

Service level management is where service level requirements as well as impact, urgency and prioritization models will be discussed and agreed to. An understanding of the IT services, the impact to those services when disruptions occur, and the urgency for resolving problems is critical to problem management. Also critical to service level management is an understanding of the potential impact on a service, or services, of a proposed resolution to a problem.

Table 4.1 Service level management: inputs to and outputs from problem management

Inputs to problem management from SLM	Outputs from problem management to SLM
Service level requirements/targets	Known errors, workarounds and solutions
Service/problem reporting requirements	Service impacts of problems and their resolutions
Information on unreported incidents	
Service level management performance metrics and achievements against service targets	Problem management performance metrics and achievements against service targets
	Closed problems and known errors
Service improvement opportunities	Findings from problem post-implementation reviews

For various reasons, business users may be living with incidents that are frequently occurring but which have not been reported to the service desk. These incidents may be indicative of an underlying problem. Service level reviews provide an opportunity for these incidents to be identified and discussed. Likewise, information from problem management pertaining to workarounds, problem closures and the need for end-user training related to permanent solutions can be part of service level review meetings.

4.1.2 Incident management

Incident management (INC) is focused on restoring service as quickly as possible to minimize the impact on business processes. In Chapter 2, we talked about incident management and its relationship to problem management in considerable depth. A problem is often triggered by one or more incidents reported to the service desk. As the incidents escalate in number and scope, they are analysed as potential problems and are considered by problem management for investigation and identification of root cause. Incidents that are linked to problem records can indicate the impact on the business and aid in prioritization of the problem.

Table 4.2 Incident management: inputs to and outputs from problem management

Inputs to problem management from INC	Outputs from problem management to INC
Incident records/details	Resolutions
Knowledge article drafts	Workarounds
Opened problem records	New/updated knowledge articles
Linkages to problem records	Scripts for incident diagnosis and resolution
Incident reports	Status updates
	Closed problems and known errors

4.1.3 Change management

Change management (CHM) controls, coordinates and approves the implementation of changes (e.g. problem solutions) to the controlled computing environments.

When problem management has identified the root cause and a permanent solution to a problem, the proposed solution often entails the modification of one or more faulty configuration items. Problem management is responsible for submitting a request for change (RFC) to change management for the approval and implementation of the proposed solution or for the workaround. In addition, if a change causes incidents, problem management may get involved to identify a workaround and/or solution to the underlying root cause of those incidents.

Table 4.3 Change management: inputs to and outputs from problem management

Inputs to problem management from CHM	Outputs from problem management to CHM
RFC status (accepted, rejected, approved, closed)	RFCs/change proposals to resolve errors
	Problem analysis
Change advisory board minutes and actions	Risk and impact analysis
Post-implementation reviews	Business cases
Failed changes that require investigation	

Change management coordinates changes to resolve open problems and known errors and ensures they are authorized, implemented and reviewed. It also keeps problem management advised of the progress of the RFC as it proceeds through the change management process.

4.1.4 Release management

Release management (RLM) is responsible for the building, testing and implementation of required changes to controlled CIs. As it relates to problem management, this would occur for the restoration of a service, be it a workaround or permanent solution. Release management coordinates the implementation of the change as described within the RFC submitted by problem management. This process is usually reserved for larger and more significant changes to the controlled environments where project management discipline is required.

There are situations when an organization might justify (based on schedule, cost or impact) moving an application or system with known bugs into production. Release management ensures that these known bugs (errors) and their workarounds are documented and that the information is transferred to the known error database or knowledge base when the application or system is moved into production.

Table 4.4 Release management: inputs to and outputs from problem management

Inputs to problem management from RLM	Outputs from problem management to RLM
Known errors and workarounds from the development and test environments	Documented problem solution
	Approval recommendation to proceed with solution build
Release policies	
Release plans	Business cases
Release status	
Post-implementation reviews	
Failed releases that require investigation	

4.1.5 Configuration management

Configuration management (CFG) identifies, records, controls, manages and reports on IT components (CIs) that are used to support delivery of agreed services to the customers. The configuration management database (CMDB) stores information about CIs. These configuration records contain attributes of the CIs and their relationships to other CIs. Typical CI categories include IT services, hardware, software, facilities, people and controlled documents such as policies, process documentation and service level agreements.

Most IT service providers use an ITSM tool that supports their ITSM process implementation efforts. This ITSM tool usually includes the capability of storing various types of data and process records, including the ability to relate a process record to another process record; a process record to a configuration record; and a configuration record to another configuration record. For example, the tool supports relating an incident record to a CI, an incident record to a problem record, a problem record to a known error record, a problem record to a change record and a change record to the CIs that are being changed.

Problem management uses the CMDB to help determine which CIs are at fault and to understand the impact of the problem and its resolution. Proactive problem management can perform a search on the CMDB to look for CIs (or CI categories) with multiple incidents or changes linked to them, which may indicate an underlying problem.

When problem management determines the root cause and the CI at fault, the problem record is linked to that CI. When the RFC is submitted to change management and the change record is created, the problem record will be linked to that change record and the change record will be linked to that same CI indicating the CI is being changed for the purpose of resolving a problem. Defining and ensuring that these inter-process and CI relationships occur is part of the configuration management process.

Table 4.5 Configuration management: inputs to and outputs from problem management

Inputs to problem management from CFG	Outputs from problem management to CFG
Configuration management system and the CMDB	Problem and known error records and their CI linkages
CIs – their attributes and relationships	Updated CI records (from the execution of approved changes)
Impact analysis reports, or query results	
Configuration management reports	

4.1.6 Knowledge management

Knowledge management (KNM) is concerned with identifying and capturing data and information that can be searched, found and used for improved decision-making throughout the organization. Its focus is to turn tacit knowledge into explicit knowledge.

Knowledge management is responsible for the building, testing, implementation and maintenance of the organization's knowledge base. The knowledge base may contain various types of information. Examples might include the answers to frequently asked questions, workarounds, automated scripts on how-tos and other information that needs to be recorded, maintained and consumed.

From a problem management perspective, the knowledge base may form the foundation for the storage of workarounds, known errors, solutions and scripts for resolving incidents and problems. Access to the knowledge base may be restricted to just IT personnel, or select information may be made available to users, when appropriate, so they can quickly find answers to their questions or solve their own incidents and problems. As stated previously, it is an organizational decision as to whether to use the knowledge base for storing workarounds and known error articles or to use the known error database. Regardless of the choice, the use of a search engine that enables information (e.g. solutions and workarounds) to be stored, found and reused is vital to incident and problem management.

Table 4.6 Knowledge management: inputs to and outputs from problem management

Inputs to problem management from KNM	Outputs from problem management to KNM
Knowledge articles: • Workarounds • Known errors • Solutions Scripts to use in diagnosing and resolving problems Training on how to use the knowledge base Knowledge article use count	New/updated knowledge articles Conclusions drawn from data and knowledge mining Application of a knowledge article

4.1.7 Financial management

Financial management (FIN) creates and maintains a framework for managing and communicating the cost and funding of IT services. Financial management activities include budgeting, accounting for expenses and costing of IT services.

Table 4.7 Financial management: inputs to and outputs from problem management

Inputs to problem management from FIN	Outputs from problem management to FIN
Approved budgets Cost models Pricing Approval or rejection of proposed solution(s)	Identified workarounds and solutions Risk, impact and costing data of different resolution options Problem and error trends Business cases

Problem management interfaces with financial management for the purpose of discussing and determining the cost and value of the different options for resolving and preventing problems.

4.1.8 Capacity management

Capacity management (CAP) focuses on the performance and use of IT services and infrastructure components in support of business processes. It is concerned with transaction volumes, response times, use thresholds and managing the resources required to deliver IT services.

Capacity management may identify problems related to services or CIs and initiate an RFC to resolve them. Likewise, problem management may engage capacity management to monitor performance of a service or CI as part of problem investigation and diagnosis activities.

Table 4.8 Capacity management: inputs to and outputs from problem management

Inputs to problem management from CAP	Outputs from problem management to CAP
Capacity plans	Known errors, workarounds and solutions
Capacity baselines	Process status updates
Capacity thresholds	Problem and error trends
Performance alerts	Requests for monitoring
System activity logs	

4.1.9 Supplier/vendor management

Supplier/vendor management (SUP) is responsible for the management of all suppliers and subcontracted suppliers and for creating, negotiating, agreeing and reviewing of all supplier-related contracts.

Remember from Chapter 1 that IT services may be provided to customers by a combination of both internal and external service providers. Many IT organizations are dependent upon an external service provider for cloud services, web hosting, or software as a service (SaaS). These are just a few examples of external IT service providers (suppliers) that are involved in delivering IT services to your customers. Because suppliers and their goods and services may be the source of problems, they will need to be involved in identification, investigation and resolution of problems related to their goods and services.

When writing contracts with suppliers, be sure to include statements within the contract that require the supplier to read, sign and date a copy of your incident, problem, change and information security management policies. These are key ITSM processes you use to support and deliver services to your customers. You should require suppliers to follow and adhere to your incident, problem, change and information security management processes when resolving incidents and problems and making changes within your controlled computing environments. This will help to ensure that all IT service providers and partners are working together effectively, consistently and predictably in delivering IT services.

Table 4.9 Supplier management: inputs to and outputs from problem management

Inputs to problem management from SUP	Outputs from problem management to SUP
Supplier contracts, agreements and targets	Supplier contract and performance issues
Supplier contact information	Identified supplier problems
Known defects or errors	Problem updates
Improvement actions and plans	Problem and error trends
Permanent solutions	Supplier tracking and performance reports
Risk and impact data	

4.1.10 Visual representations of process interactions

Figure 4.1 provides a visual representation of process interactions. When we first developed this figure there was considerable discussion regarding how much detail to include. As we have used this diagram now in numerous training scenarios, it has proved of great value as we see light bulbs turn on with regard to process workflow and process interdependencies.

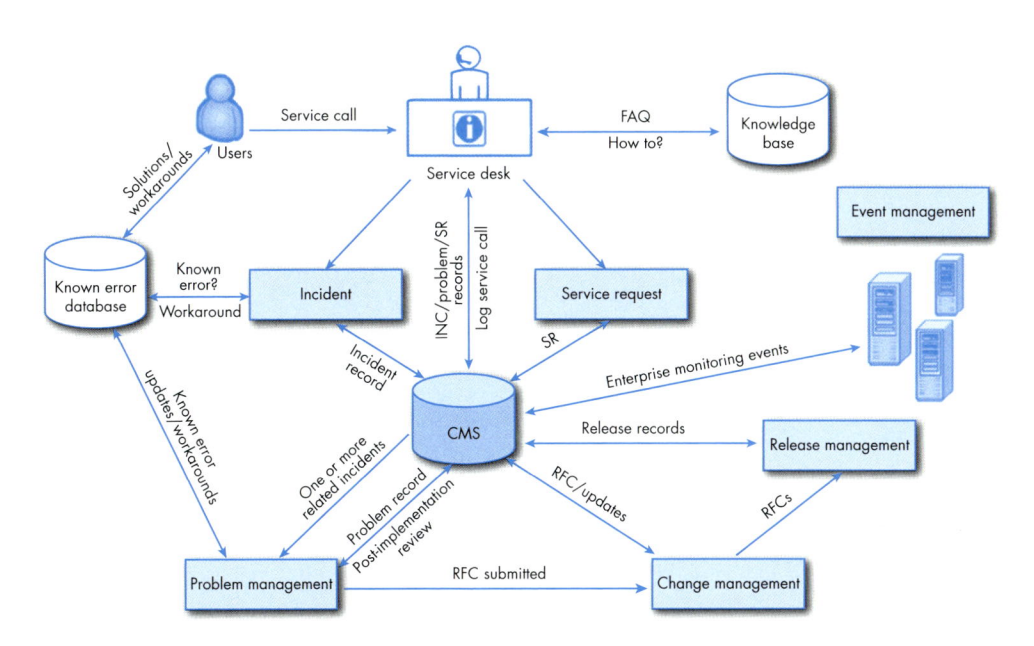

Figure 4.1 Relationships between ITSM processes, users and the service desk function (other relationships not shown)

Figure 4.1 can be explained as follows:

- A user has experienced an incident and needs help from IT. The user can look for a workaround or solution in the known error database (or knowledge base) and if found, apply it to quickly solve the incident for themselves. For self-reported incidents (e.g. via a web interface), some ITSM tools will allow the user to apply a workaround or solution to an incident by clicking a 'Use' button. The use count can be queried to determine how many times the workaround or solution has been used. This use count can be used by proactive problem management to identify a potential underlying problem.

- If the user contacts the service desk for assistance, the service desk will first enquire about the nature of the call. It may be the call is a need for information or instruction on how to perform a certain task. In that case, the service desk agent might query the knowledge base, looking for the answer to their request. In many organizations, the user has access to the knowledge base to perform this query themselves. When the call is a request for information or for a service, the agent would log it as a service request to be handled by the organization's request fulfilment process.

- Otherwise, the agent logs an incident and then searches for documented workarounds and solutions. If found, the agent provides the workaround or solution to the caller. If one was not found, the agent will try to resolve it by performing investigation and diagnosis of the incident.

- When one or more related incidents have occurred, a problem record may be opened (based on the organizational criteria established for when a problem record is opened). Problem management will then work to identify the root cause, a workaround and a permanent solution. If the root cause and a workaround are identified, a known error record is created and the status of the problem record is changed to a known error. The workaround is then stored within the problem record, known error record, or knowledge base article, dependent on decisions made by the organization as to where to store workarounds.

- When problem management has identified, developed and tested (when possible) a permanent solution, an RFC is submitted to change management to gain solution implementation approval.

- Depending on the nature of the change, problem management will work with change and release management to implement the solution.

- Once the solution is implemented, a post-implementation review is conducted to confirm it did indeed fix the problem. If successful, the problem record is closed, along with any remaining open incidents linked to the problem.

- Throughout all of the above activities and tasks, configuration management updates the configuration management system (CMS) and CMDB to reflect changes and relationships between the processes and changed CIs.

Problem management relationships

- Event management may identify events of significance and initiate the activities above by creating an incident record within the CMS. The incident record may be for a service-disrupting event or one where services and users have not yet been impacted. The incident record may be indicative of an underlying problem where problem management can be engaged to perform root cause analysis and take corrective actions.

Now let's use a swim lane diagram as shown in Figure 4.2 to illustrate problem management process relationships. The diagram is explained as follows:

- An incident may be identified in several different ways:
    - Event, availability, or capacity management monitoring of the infrastructure detects an event that requires an incident to be logged
    - A user or support person detects an incident.
- Regardless of how the incident was detected, it initiates the recording of an incident.

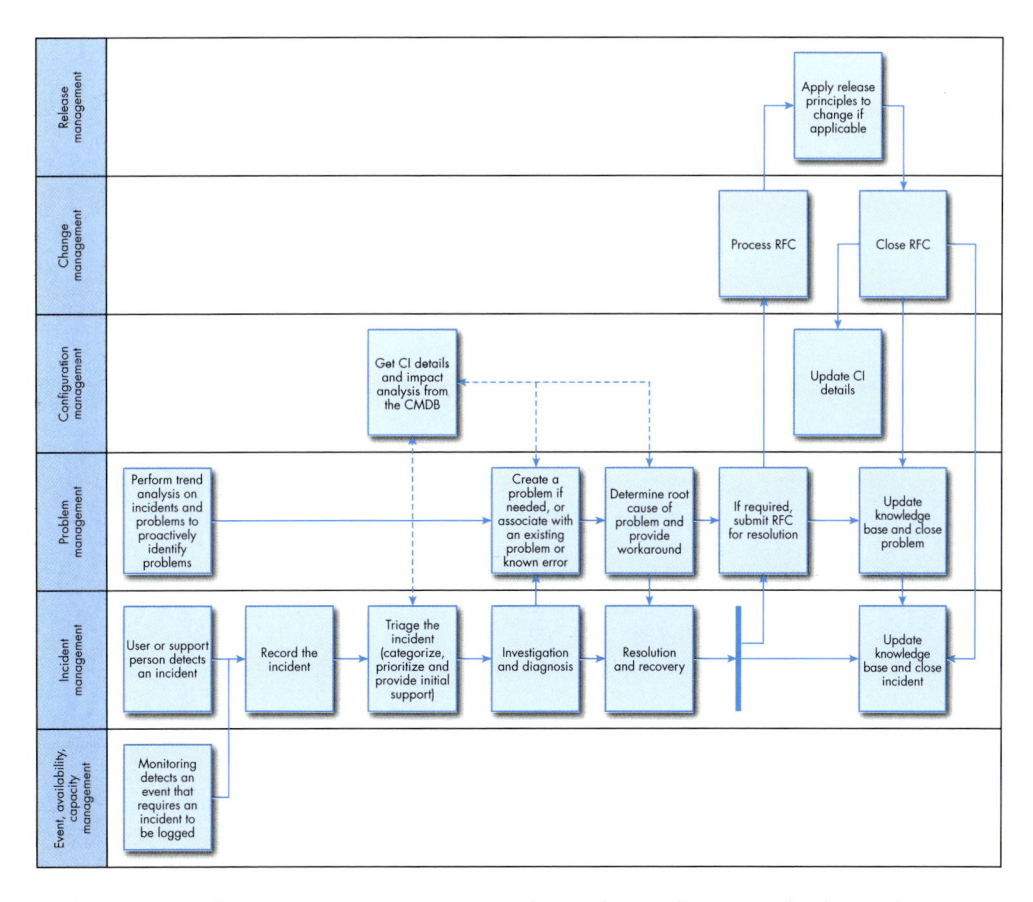

Figure 4.2 Problem management process relationships (all potential relationships not shown)

- Triage is where the incident is categorized and prioritized and resources are allocated to provide initial support.
- The next step is to perform incident investigation and diagnosis. If it is determined during this activity that a problem record needs to be opened, follow the arrow up to the next level (problem management swim lane) and create a problem record, then link the incident record to the problem record.
- Continuing along the problem management swim lane, the next activity is to determine the problem's root cause and provide a workaround, or better workaround, for incident management.
- When a solution (or a workaround) is identified, submit a request for change to change management (when necessary) to seek approval for the implementation of the solution. Sometimes the permanent solution to a problem is resolved by improving communications or training personnel. In those cases, the submission of an RFC to change management may not be necessary.
- If the change is large or complex enough, release management disciplines will be followed to implement the change.
- Once a permanent solution is implemented and confirmed as successful, the next steps are to close the change record, update CI details in the CMDB, update the knowledge base and close the problem record.
- When the problem record is closed, any open incidents related to the problem are closed and their resolutions are reported to the customer.

Note that some of the activities above may be initiated by proactive problem management where technical support groups have performed trend analysis on incidents or other data and have identified a problem. Known defects and errors from suppliers may also initiate these activities.

4.2 Problem management's relationship to ITSM functions

We defined functions and described functional teams in Chapter 1. Our focus in this section is on the relationship between ITSM functions and problem management.

We defined functional teams as units of organizations specialized to perform certain types of work and to be responsible for specific outcomes. We went on to say that these functional teams are often referred to as technical support groups and are typically defined by the technology domains they support. In addition, there are other functional teams that are not necessarily technical but are instead customer-facing and operational in nature.

Functional teams can vary significantly in number, size, capabilities and responsibilities based on the location of the teams, size of the organization, organizational culture and the technologies that are employed in the delivery of IT services. Frequently there will be an overlap between these functional teams due to organizational size or operational constraints. For example, the service desk may only be staffed Monday through Friday from 8 a.m. to 5 p.m. After 5 p.m. and on weekends, calls to the service desk may roll over and be handled by the IT operations area, which is often staffed 24 × 7 × 365.

Because IT organizations vary from one to another, the organization of functional teams into units with assigned responsibilities also varies by organization. Table 4.10 is a summarized list of IT functional teams and how they might be organized into broad categories.

Table 4.10 Examples of functional teams

Functional category	Functional teams
Infrastructure	Application development/management
	Database
	Enterprise architecture
	Middleware
	Network
	Security administration
	Server
	Storage
	Telecom
	Web
Customer-facing	Business relationship office
	Desktop support
	ITSM programme office
	Project management office
	Service desk
Operations	IT operations
	Network operations centre
	Production control

Members of these teams can be assigned to specific roles and perform various activities and tasks within several different ITSM processes. From a service restoration perspective, functional teams can identify, log, categorize and resolve incidents, which in turn supports the identification and logging of problems.

We stated in Chapter 2 that many IT organizations refer to their functional teams in 'tiers'. Tier 1 personnel are often referred to as the service desk. Tier 2 personnel are typically the junior level staff within the technical support groups while Tier 3 personnel are the more senior staff. Tier 2 personnel are most often involved in resolving incidents and linking

Table 4.11 Inputs to and outputs from problem management by functional category

Category	Inputs to problem management	Outputs from problem management
Infrastructure	Logged and categorized incidents Problem records Workarounds Resolution actions taken Knowledge articles Linkages to problems, known errors or knowledge base articles Known errors and workarounds from the development and test environments or from suppliers System/application logs, journals and monitoring reports Risk assessment and analysis Technical knowledge and skills	Known errors, workarounds and solutions Status updates on problems and known errors New/updated knowledge articles Scripts for incident and problem diagnosis and resolution Closed problems and known errors Service achievements against service targets Service improvement opportunities and plans Service impacts on problems and their resolutions
Customer-facing	Logged and categorized incidents Problem records Workarounds Resolution actions taken Knowledge articles Linkages to problems, known errors or knowledge base articles Customer knowledge and communication skills User feedback Specifications and requirements Assistance on problem prioritization and the business case for resolution Service performance and achievements against targets Information on potential problems	Known errors, workarounds and solutions Status updates on problems and known errors New/updated knowledge articles Scripts for incident and problem diagnosis and resolution Closed problems and known errors Service achievements against service targets Service improvement opportunities and plans Process improvement opportunities
Operations	Logged and categorized incidents Problem records Workarounds Resolution actions taken Knowledge articles Linkages to problems, known errors or knowledge base articles Service performance and achievements against targets Information on potential problems	Known errors, workarounds and solutions Status updates on problems and known errors New/updated knowledge articles Scripts for incident and problem diagnosis and resolution Closed problems and known errors

incidents to problems, to known error records or to knowledge base articles. While Tier 3 personnel may also be assigned incidents, they are usually responsible for the creation of problem records, resolution and the identification of incident trends and patterns that may be indicative of a problem. In some organizations, service desk and IT operations functions may be delegated the responsibility of opening problem records or requesting one be opened by technical support personnel.

Table 4.11 provides a summary of the inputs to, and outputs from problem management for the three functional categories shown in Table 4.10.

5 Organizing for problem management

In this chapter we will describe the roles specific to the problem management process. We will also explain and provide a problem management RACI model – an authority, responsibility and communication matrix often used to map roles and responsibilities in relation to a process and its activities. We will end the chapter by talking about different organizational models for allocating staff for the performance of problem management activities.

There are three primary roles that support problem management. For each of these roles we will provide a description, a listing of their responsibilities, the skills and knowledge needed and suggested training. In addition to the three primary roles there are several complementary roles that interface with and support the problem management process. We will provide a brief explanation of these complementary roles and their responsibilities. Note that in some organizations these roles may not exist, are called something else, or there may be more than one person filling a role. In a smaller organization, one person may be assigned multiple roles.

Before we begin, we need to define and clarify the difference between a role and a job description:

- **Role** A role is the description of the responsibilities, skills and tasks executed as part of a defined process – a 'process assignment'. Roles are used to assign the execution of one or more process tasks in a structured way. A process will not be effective until someone (or something) is performing the activities in each role. Note that roles may change if the process owner changes the design or execution of the process.

- **Job description** A job description is a structured description of the assumed contribution a person will make to the overall goals of an organization. Its purpose is to allow for equitable payment within the organization for a defined set of skills and experience. Job descriptions are typically owned by the personnel or human resources department.

> **Note**
> There is a difference between a functional role and a process role. As an example, a Windows engineer performs a function related to server management, but this same engineer may be assigned one or more process roles, in one or more processes.

The following sections contain descriptions of the process roles needed to support the problem management process.

5.1 Roles and responsibilities

The three primary roles associated with problem management are the process owner, problem manager and problem analyst.

5.1.1 Process owner

As stated previously, every process should have a process owner. The problem management process owner maintains, measures and governs the process, ensuring the process is meeting the business needs, is followed by the organization, and that process compliance exceptions are addressed. The process owner is accountable for the coordination and implementation of process improvement initiatives and for ensuring that process documentation and training material are maintained. This role would usually be performed by a senior IT manager within the organization, because having hierarchical and positional authority is critical to the role.

5.1.1.1 Responsibilities

The responsibilities of the problem management process owner are to:

- Collaborate with stakeholders to define and agree on process requirements, priorities, performance levels and management information requirements
- Provide input to, and approve, the process design and scope
- Review and approve the documentation of the process, standards and standard operating procedures (SOPs) to be used throughout the process
- Provide motivation and inspiration to help build a supportive process environment
- Approve the problem management automation and tool requirements
- Act as the escalation point for dealing with process compliance issues
- Provide a common vision and direction
- Ensure education (knowledge transfer), training (skill transfer) and communication systems are developed and implemented
- Ensure interfaces with other processes are working effectively
- Ensure critical success factors (CSFs) and key performance indicators (KPIs) are measuring the effectiveness and efficiency of the process
- Review KPIs and initiate improvement action(s) based on KPI analysis
- Measure and report on compliance with process policies and standards
- Interface with line management, ensuring that the process receives the necessary staff resources
- Mentor and coach problem managers.

5.1.1.2 Skills and knowledge required

The problem management process owner should be able to demonstrate:

- In-depth knowledge of the business and how IT supports business needs
- In-depth knowledge of the problem management process, activities and interfaces to other processes
- Customer service skills
- Collaborative and consensus-building skills
- Ability to coach and mentor individual contributors
- In-depth knowledge of the IT department and its structure and culture
- Infrastructure and application support knowledge
- Conflict resolution skills
- Negotiation and facilitation skills.

5.1.1.3 Suggested training

The problem management process owner should have an advanced level of ITSM training in service restoration.

5.1.2 Problem manager

The process manager for problem management is referred to as the problem manager. The problem manager is often appointed by, or at least approved by, the process owner and can be a functional leader at the level at which the physical work of the process is accomplished. The problem manager will sit on the process design team and have decision-making responsibility regarding the design and implementation of the process.

Once the process is implemented, the problem manager is responsible for monitoring compliance with the process and the health of the process. He or she acts as the 'eyes and ears' of the process owner, providing information to the process owner on the daily performance of the process.

5.1.2.1 Responsibilities

The responsibilities of the problem manager are to:

- Develop and maintain the problem management process and supporting documentation
- Ensure the investigation of problems
- Advise incident management staff of workarounds and resolved problems
- Identify training requirements for the process and tools; ensure knowledge transfer and assist in the delivery of training
- Ensure target resolution times are met

- Act as the control point for process and quality controls within the process
- Ensure the production of required management reports
- Coordinate the organization's response to major problems by leading a problem resolution team
- Recommend changes to the design and scope of the process
- Assist in securing required resources to perform problem management activities
- Address and resolve issues with process operation and execution
- Guide and assist support group staff in developing and delivering workarounds and resolutions; act as a mentor and coach
- Monitor progress on resolving known errors
- Ensure problems are documented properly
- Ensure sufficient communication is provided to the customer, including progress statements
- Participate in major incident meetings and reviews
- Participate in, oversee and review the effectiveness of proactive problem management activities
- Identify process improvements.

5.1.2.2 Skills and knowledge required

The problem manager should be able to demonstrate:

- In-depth knowledge of the services that IT delivers to customers
- In-depth knowledge of the service management tools used to support the process
- Ability to explain and guide staff through the process
- Teamwork/team-building skills
- Effective meeting facilitation skills
- Knowledge of customer needs and service level agreements
- Knowledge of the technical environment
- In-depth knowledge of the process workflow, CSFs and KPIs
- In-depth knowledge of how problem management interfaces with other processes
- Oral and written communication skills
- Analytical and trend analysis skills
- Resource management skills
- Knowledge of root cause analysis techniques.

5.1.2.3 Suggested training

The problem manager should:

- Be trained in the use of ITSM tools
- Be trained to use root cause analysis techniques
- Have an advanced level of ITSM training in service restoration.

5.1.3 Problem analyst

The problem analyst role is synonymous with the process analyst role we described in Chapter 1, only specific to problem management. Individuals in this role are usually, but not always, internal technical support staff responsible for providing Tier 2 and Tier 3 support for the IT infrastructure.

Problem analysts are assigned problem records and are responsible for carrying out problem management process activities. From a proactive problem management perspective, they are responsible for creating, categorizing and prioritizing problem records as a result of monitoring the infrastructure, and for performing analysis of system logs, journals and incidents, looking for trends and patterns that indicate an underlying problem. They are also responsible for creating knowledge articles and/or opening problem records for supplier defects in their respective areas of expertise.

5.1.3.1 Responsibilities

The responsibilities of the problem analyst are to:

- Acknowledge and work on assigned problem records
- Track assigned problem and known error records; update the record with newly discovered information according to process guidelines and timeframes
- Create a known error record (or knowledge article) when a root cause and workaround have been identified
- Involve required resources from other support groups to determine root cause, workarounds and/or permanent solutions
- Create problem records based on interpretation and trending of alerts, events and incidents
- Submit requests for change (RFCs) to resolve problems and known errors
- Ensure that sufficient communication is provided to the customer, including progress updates on the problem
- Communicate and train service desk staff on new or updated workarounds, or on existing workarounds that staff are not executing well
- Determine and document the root cause of problem records through the use of root cause analysis techniques

- Document workarounds within the problem record, known error database or knowledge base
- Inform the problem manager of any impediments to the problem analyst's effectiveness in supporting problem management and/or resolving problems
- Test each identified resolution or workaround
- Create problem records, known errors and knowledge articles based on vendor defects
- Work with supplier and vendor support groups to resolve problems.

5.1.3.2 Skills and knowledge required

The problem analyst should be able to demonstrate:

- In-depth knowledge of the process workflow and supporting documentation
- In-depth knowledge of how problem management interfaces with other processes
- Analytical and problem-solving skills
- Knowledge of root cause analysis techniques
- Understanding of incident, change and configuration management
- In-depth knowledge of the service management tools used to support the process
- Strong technical proficiency
- Written documentation skills
- Knowledge of the technical environment.

5.1.3.3 Suggested training

The problem analyst should:

- Be trained in the use of ITSM tools
- Be able to use root cause analysis techniques
- Have undergone detailed process training on incident, problem, change and configuration management.

5.1.4 Complementary roles

In Chapter 4, we described the relationship of problem management to several different ITSM processes and IT functions. There are a number of roles within these processes and functions that will either interface with, or support, problem management activities. We refer to these as complementary roles.

Table 5.1 provides a list of the more commonly found complementary roles and a summary of their responsibilities to problem management.

Table 5.1 Complementary roles supporting problem management

Role	Responsibilities
Incident manager	Ensures incident data is logged and categorized correctly for use by problem management
	Ensures problem records are appropriately opened from the incident management process using the established organizational criteria for opening a problem record
	Leads the organization's response to major incidents, including any required hand-overs to problem management
	Ensures incidents are appropriately linked to problem records
Knowledge manager	Designs the procedures around knowledge capture and management for use by the problem management process
	Works with problem management staff to develop scripts, create knowledge articles and publish approved articles
	Ensures the knowledge base is available and kept up to date by the responsible owners of the knowledge articles
Change manager	Receives and processes RFCs submitted from problem management for the purpose of resolving problems and known errors
	Ensures RFCs submitted for implementation are presented to the appropriate level of authority for approval
	Communicates change status to problem management
Service desk manager	Works with problem management staff to provide timely and appropriate communications to stakeholders on the status of problems
	Ensures open incidents that are linked to a 'Closed' problem record are also closed
	Ensures service desk staffing levels are adequate to perform problem management tasks assigned to their role
Service owner	Responsible for one or more IT services and represents the service to customers across the organization
	Works with the business relationship manager in building and communicating the business case for the identified problem workaround or permanent solution
Business relationship manager	Responsible for ensuring the service provider understands the customer and their business needs and how services are being offered and delivered
Report specialist	Works with stakeholders and the problem manager to create and produce actionable problem management KPI and management reports
	Ensures consistency and accuracy of data between problem management and other process reports

5.1.5 Adapting process roles in your organization

When your organization 'adopts' a problem management process, you will need to adapt it to your organization. Now that we have explained the primary and complementary roles associated with problem management, you may be asking, 'How do we adapt these roles to our company's version of the process?' 'How do we go about filling these roles within our organization?'

The following steps are useful when adapting these roles to existing staff positions within your organization:

- Discuss the pros and cons of the set of proposed roles for problem management
- Identify any needed changes in the list of problem management and complementary roles
- For each role, update (adapt) the set of responsibilities to your organization
- For each role in the adapted set:
    - Identify (map) who is or should be performing the role within your company today
    - Identify gaps in responsibilities: what is in the adapted responsibility list that is not being performed by the mapped resources today?
    - Identify and eliminate overlaps in responsibilities (duplication of effort)
    - Identify implications and obstacles that would make it difficult to implement these roles at your company
    - Identify plans and implement solutions to close the gaps and overcome the obstacles.

5.2 RACI matrix

We said at the beginning of this chapter that a RACI matrix is an authority matrix often used to map roles and responsibilities in relation to a process and its tasks. As explained below, RACI stands for Responsible, Accountable, Consulted, Informed. We recommend you develop a RACI matrix for every ITSM process you design and implement.

Creation of a RACI matrix is sometimes called 'RACI charting'. RACI charting is a systematic technique to:

- Identify all the process tasks that have to be accomplished for effective operation of the process
- Clarify roles and individual levels of participation in relation to each process task
- Establish communication requirements prior to and after task completion.

A RACI matrix provides a framework for governance of the process that results in increased productivity through the elimination of overlaps and redundancies in staff assignments. Staff

Organizing for problem management

(role) expectations for process tasks are explicitly identified, resulting in less confusion, fewer misunderstandings and improved organizational effectiveness.

Benefits or outcomes of using a RACI matrix include:

- Assigning task-by-task participation requirements as a function of process role
- Clarifying roles and responsibilities across functional teams
- Assigning accountability for tasks
- Establishing responsibility for tasks
- Obtaining buy-in across the organization
- Ensuring appropriate staff are consulted and informed.

What does the acronym RACI stand for?

- **R**esponsible for performing the task. These are the roles that actually complete the task and are responsible for correct execution of the task. Responsibility is often shared, with each role's degree of responsibility determined by the role that is assigned the 'A' for the task.
- **A**ccountable for the outcome – definitive ownership. This is the role that carries the 'yes' or 'no' authority and has full veto power for an activity. Only one role can be assigned the 'A' for a task. Authority must accompany accountability.
- **C**onsulted for input before an action. These are the roles that may be consulted for information, knowledge or opinions prior to a final decision or action. 'Consulted' implies two-way communication.
- **I**nformed for knowledge after an action. These are the roles that need to be informed after a decision or action is taken because they, in turn, may take action or make a decision based on the task's output. 'Informed' implies one-way communication. Identifying which roles should be assigned the 'I' is based on the determination of roles that may be directly impacted by, or have a stake in, the outcome of the process tasks.

A high-level RACI matrix example for problem management activities can be seen in Table 5.2. Note that the process owner has accountability for the overall process and, as such, is not represented at the process activity or task level.

The following steps can be used when developing your RACI matrix:

- Document the activities and tasks that make up the process (see Appendix C)
- Identify the functional and process roles associated with the process
- Hold a workshop to discuss and assign the RACI letters

Table 5.2 Simplified RACI matrix for problem management

Problem management activities	Problem manager	Problem analyst	Service desk	Knowledge manager	Change manager	Release manager	Report specialist	Stakeholders (includes suppliers)
Detection	A, R, C	R, C	R					R, I
Logging	A, R, C, I	R, C, I	R, I					I
Investigation and diagnosis	A, R, C	R, C	C	C, I				R, C
Resolution	A, R, C, I	R, C, I	I		R, C, I	R, C		R, C, I
Closure	A, R	I	I					I
Major problem review	A, R	C	C					C
Proactive problem management	A, R	R, C, I	C, I					C, I
Problem reporting	A, R, C, I	C, I	I				R, C	I

- Place accountability (A) and responsibility (R) at the lowest feasible level (i.e. delegate down the organizational hierarchy as much as is practical), where:
  - It's OK for one role to have both A and R for a task
  - There can only be one role with the A per task
  - Authority must accompany accountability
- Optimize the number of consults (Cs) and informs (Is).

Note that it is not required that every task has a C or an I. Once the matrix has been completed, check and correct for the following:

- **R** Are there too many Rs assigned to a specific role? Are there too many roles assigned Rs for this task (therefore no one takes responsibility)? Is at least one role assigned an R for each task?
- **A** Is one and only one A assigned per task? Should someone else be accountable for this task?
- **C and I** Are there too many roles assigned a C or I (which could result in too much discussion and slow the process down), or are there too few Cs or Is (an indication that communication may not be occurring enough)?
- Do some roles have too many tasks?

The RACI matrix should be revisited regularly to determine if any changes are necessary and to prevent role confusion. A description and explanation of the matrix and its use should be included in the process training provided to all individuals associated with the process.

5.3 Organizational models

> **Fitting it all in**
> Organizations are constantly being asked to do more with existing, or even fewer resources. A typical workday for an IT staff member consists of daily operational and maintenance activities for those configuration items for which they are responsible; receiving and responding to incidents, service requests and phone calls; attending meetings; performing administrative tasks; and completing project work. As a functional team member, you may be thinking, 'I already have a full-time job. How do I fit problem management activities into my day?' Or, if you're a manager, 'How do I organize and allocate staff to perform problem management activities when we already have more work than our staff can complete?'

When we talk about **organizing** for problem management, we are not talking about reorganizing for problem management, although a degree of this may occur depending on the organizational model chosen to perform problem management. This isn't about how to change functional organizational charts, but rather how to allocate resources and logically organize them to perform problem management activities, which are often performed inefficiently or possibly not at all. And, by the way, we are talking about process roles here, not functional roles or job descriptions.

Figure 5.1 represents a typical organizational structure that smaller IT organizations can adopt for performing problem management activities. Note that in very small organizations, a single individual may perform the activities of the process owner, process manager and perhaps even the problem analyst.

In Figure 5.1, we have a process owner, a problem manager and problem analysts who reside within the various technical support groups. You will recall that the process manager for problem management is referred to as the problem manager. Here we see that there are no direct reporting relationships; instead we have indirect or matrixed relationships denoted by the dotted lines.

Given this structure, the organization will assign an individual to the role of the problem management process owner. That person is accountable for the overall design, implementation and performance of the process. The organization will also designate an individual to the role of the problem manager. This individual will be responsible for daily operational management of the process and for ensuring compliance with the process. The problem manager will work with the process owner to plan, coordinate and ensure all process activities are carried out. These two roles represent the governance committee in this model. Their purpose and responsibility is to govern the process, to perform quality control on process execution and to initiate process improvements.

The problem manager is responsible for assessing incidents to determine if an underlying problem exists and, if so, open a problem record; determine the skills needed to perform root cause analysis; assign the problem record to a specific problem analyst within one of the technical teams; and monitor progression of the problems to known errors and permanent fixes.

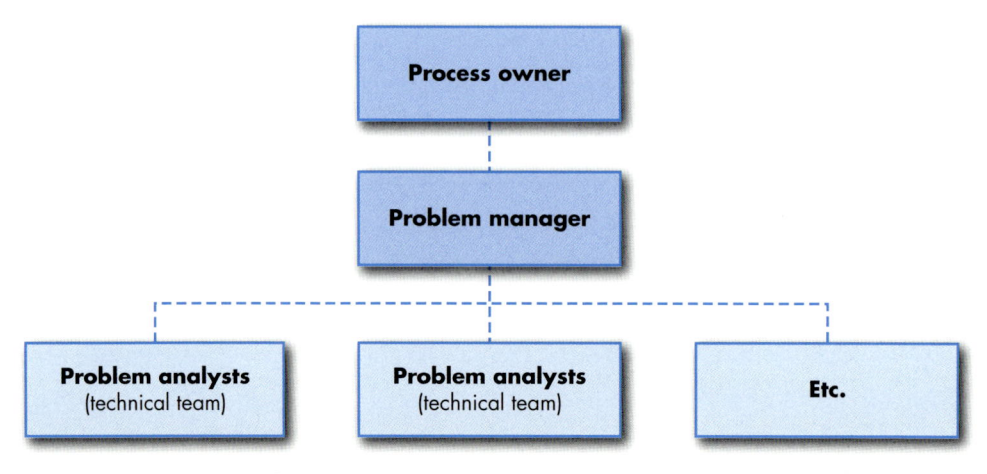

Figure 5.1 Organizing for problem management in smaller IT organizations

Organizing for problem management

This model is well-suited for small, centrally located organizations as the cost to implement is low. However, as with any model relying on indirect reporting relationships, the effectiveness and efficiency of process task execution will tend to deteriorate in the absence of strong governance and/or conflicting demands.

Figure 5.2 represents a typical organizational structure that larger IT organizations adopt for performing problem management activities.

As in Figure 5.1, Figure 5.2 has a process owner, problem manager and multiple problem analysts. But an additional role has been added – the problem queue managers – with dotted-line reporting relationships to the problem manager. Notice a solid line reporting relationship between the problem manager and the process owner, as well as between the problem analysts and problem queue managers.

In this scenario, for each of the functional technical teams an individual is assigned the role of a problem queue manager. Often, these problem queue managers are either the supervisor of the technical team or a senior technical lead within the team. As noted, each problem queue manager has a dotted-line reporting relationship to the individual fulfilling the role of the problem manager. Here, the problem manager is responsible for the daily execution of the problem management process across all the technical teams.

This structure works well for larger organizations as it provides problem queue managers with the hierarchical and positional authority needed to allocate resources, assign problems, ensure progress and effect timely outcomes. It also enables teams to focus their attention on those problems for which they are best suited for determining root cause and a permanent fix. The problem queue managers monitor their team's work queue for any open yet unassigned problem records, review them for the required skill set and then assign them. In essence, they are responsible for making sure their work-group members adhere to the full lifecycle of the problem management process.

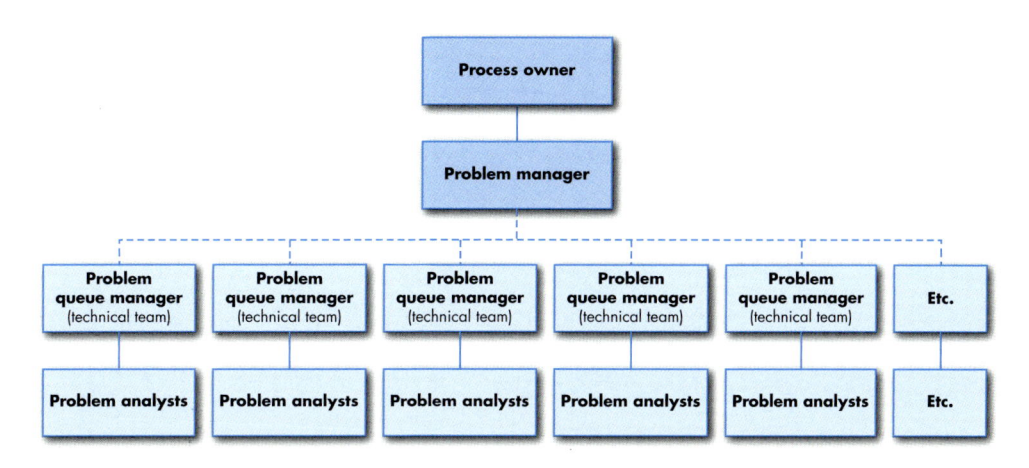

Figure 5.2 Organizing for problem management in larger IT organizations

103

Another benefit to this structure is that the problem queue manager and the problem manager can both focus on their areas of expertise. The problem queue managers are familiar with the technology supported by their technical team members and they speak the same technical lingo. This enables the problem queue managers to better assist and support the problem analysts as they perform root cause analysis and identify permanent fixes. Likewise, the problem manager focuses on the performance and success of the overall process and helps the problem queue managers be successful in their role.

> **Note**
> This organizational structure is best suited for larger organizations that have strong cross-functional team collaboration and cooperation. Without this collaboration, successful process task execution must rely on an effective governance framework.

One potential downside to this organizational structure is the balancing of workload for the problem queue managers where one may be swamped with problems to investigate or resolve, and others may have few, if any. To address this issue, some organizations implement a problem governance board, or PGB. It is comprised of the process owner, the problem manager and the problem queue managers, and is chaired by the problem manager. The PGB is a forum for:

- Determining resource allocation
- Resolving conflicts and issues
- Overcoming parochialism and narrow-mindedness
- Determining which problems to investigate (especially proactively identified problems)
- Determining which problems to pursue resolution for
- Giving approval for the closure of a problem
- Translating enterprise objectives into process goals (i.e. goal alignment)
- Reviewing KPIs and metrics.

Figure 5.3 represents another logical structure for problem management. It is the centralized model.

In the centralized problem management model, there is a dedicated centralized team that performs root cause analysis for all problems that occur, regardless of the nature of the problem or the underlying technology that may be at fault.

As there is a dedicated team, all of the reporting relationships are solid line rather than dotted line. Problem management is all this team does. This model would typically be used in large organizations that have a wide range of services with high availability requirements. A variation of this model may be implemented by organizations that use similar technologies,

Organizing for problem management

Process owner

Problem manager

Problem analysts
(various technical skills)

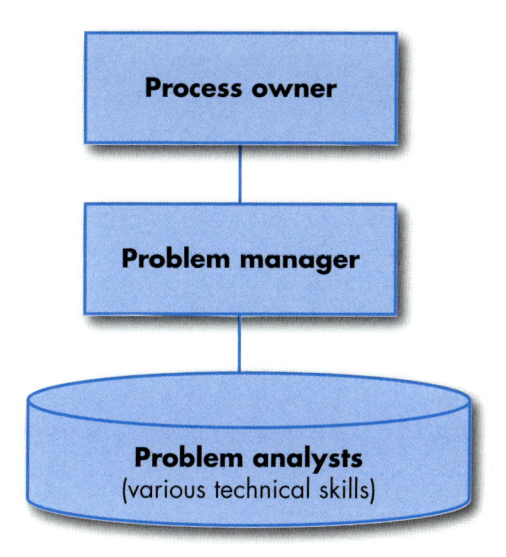

Figure 5.3 Centralized problem management organization

but have a distributed presence or multiple business subsidiaries. This model can be adapted to work globally, with considerations given to language differences and/or global workflow support hand-overs.

As with the other models, there is an individual assigned the role of the process owner and another assigned the role of the problem manager. In this model, the problem manager also performs the role of the problem queue manager. Our experience has shown this model brings increased team performance, higher-quality results and reduced likelihood of a technical silo mentality.

The final organizational model we will look at is called the task force. This logical model is represented by Figure 5.4.

In the task force model, a team of problem analysts with specific technical skills is formed to address a particular problem, area of instability or service unavailability. The team is dedicated to the problem for the duration that the problem remains unsolved, and the team's activities are defined and run as a project with clear objectives and an end date for completion. Once the problem is solved, the team may move on to another problem, or be disbanded.

This structure uses the capabilities and specialisms of technical staff with limited management oversight. Though not shown, there is indeed a process owner, with the problem manager having a dotted-line reporting relationship to the process owner. As with the centralized model, the performance of the team and the quality of the output produced is generally very high and technology silos are avoided.

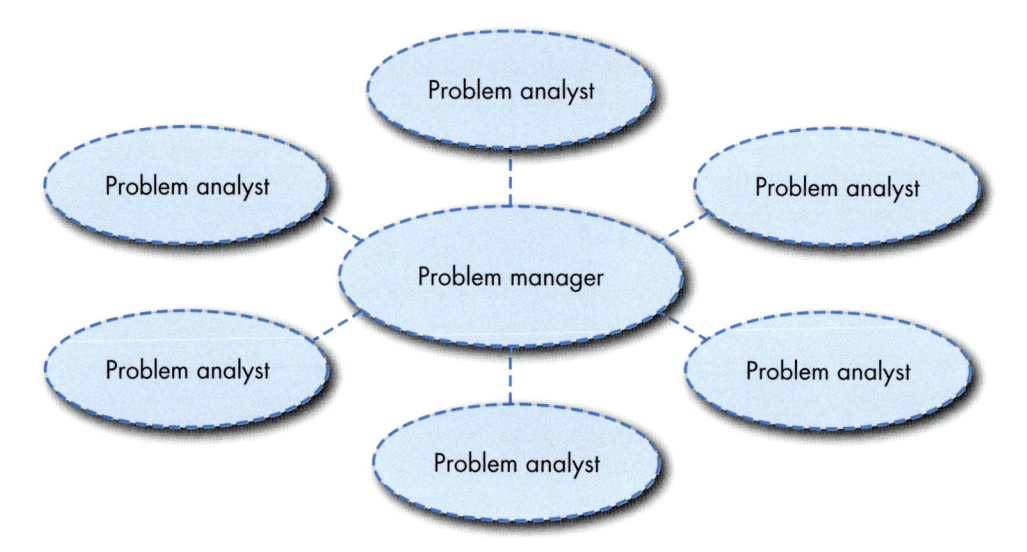

Figure 5.4 The task force organizational model

5.4 Tips on allocating resources

5.4.1 Get started

As IT organizations become more mature, less time and fewer resources are needed for fire-fighting and reacting to incidents. This is largely the result of a commitment to fix incidents permanently. With less time spent fire-fighting, those same resources may now be allocated to the problem management activities, further increasing stability by reducing incident volume, and preventing incidents from recurring. Frequently the best advice for organizations that are just getting started with problem management is to 'start simply, but simply start'. This could be accomplished by allocating staff to problem management activities for one hour a day, one day a week, one week a month, or some other time-allocation scenario. The solution could be as simple as one person performing problem management activities, or could involve several members of the IT staff.

5.4.2 Segregate your time

Regardless of the size of your IT department, time should be set aside for performing problem management activities and that time should be segregated from incident management activities. On this point, it is seldom a good idea to have the incident process manager be the same person as the problem process manager. The reason is the person's time and focus will almost always be spent on reacting to incidents, and little time will be available to spend on root cause analysis and fixing those incidents permanently.

5.4.3 Important considerations

Regardless of how you decide to organize and execute problem management activities, it is important to ensure that:

- Process governance is established and governance responsibilities are executed, including:
    - Oversight by process owner/process manager/problem queue manager
    - Timely and appropriate assignment of problems
    - Process compliance enforcement – ensuring that people are performing their problem management responsibilities correctly
- Staff are suitably trained on root cause analysis techniques
- Tight integration and collaboration of technical support groups exist, especially between applications and operations (DevOps).

6 Measuring problem management

Most IT organizations measure and report on operational activities, key initiatives and goal attainment status. Sometimes the sheer volume of reports created on a daily, weekly or quarterly basis can be overwhelming. In these IT organizations, reports are pushed to pre-established and broad distribution lists; reports are posted to SharePoint® sites or the intranet; dashboards are updated in near-real time; and countless ad hoc reports are emailed to individuals for 'action'. It seems that nearly everything IT does is measured, tracked, monitored, analysed or benchmarked. In other IT organizations little if any measurement and reporting occurs. In still others, measurements and reports are used simply as a way of proving that tasks are being accomplished, or that assignees are performing what they were assigned to do. In these cases, measurements and reports can result in 'negative work', where time and effort are wasted creating reports simply to justify actions or to defend past decisions.

How can measurement and reporting add the most value without wasting resources or causing distraction? What should be measured, and for what purpose? It's important to answer these questions generally, but also, of course, specifically for problem management reports.

6.1 Why measure?

The purpose of measuring is to help an organization focus its time, energy and resources on those things that matter most for success. Measurements are used to show an organization's progress towards achievement of its goals, objectives and commitments. They can also be used to identify weaknesses and opportunities to improve or invest in people, processes or technology.

When seeking to improve an existing product or process, attention is normally focused in three areas: cost, quality and speed to delivery, or in other words, cheaper, better and faster. Do you need to reduce cost, do you need to make improvements in quality, or do you need to deliver the products and services faster? It may be all three.

The purpose of measuring a process is to determine its overall health in terms of:

- Progress (towards a goal)
- Efficiency (speed to delivery)
- Effectiveness (cost and quality)
- Compliance (governance).

Process efficiency and effectiveness measurements guide process execution towards outcomes that produce value. That said, being effective should be the first priority. In other words, meet the objectives first and then focus on getting faster at delivering on those objectives. After all, what value is it to do 'bad' even faster?

6.1.1 Measure what?

William Bruce Cameron said, 'Not everything that can be counted counts, and not everything that counts can be counted'.[3] There is also a popular business adage that states, 'You can't control what you can't manage. You can't manage what you can't measure. And you can't measure what you can't define.' William Deming, whom we've spoken of before, said there are many important things that must be managed, but can't be measured. There is wisdom in each of these sayings.

Several books have been written on the topic of improving services and process performance through measurements. In fact, ITIL has dedicated an entire publication and process to this topic entitled *ITIL Continual Service Improvement*.[4]

For something to be worth measuring there must be value derived from the measurement. That value comes from the positive effect the information has on decisions and behaviour. Rather than focusing on what can be measured, let's focus on what is meaningful.

What is meaningful varies from organization to organization. But how to determine what is meaningful follows a general prescription. Here are the common steps:

- Define the vision: 'What are we trying to accomplish?' 'What will "done" look like?'
- Define the goals and key objectives that are aligned with the vision. These should be supported by critical success factors.
- Develop questions that will indicate whether the goals and objectives are being achieved (defining what you will measure). These are referred to as key performance indicators.
- Identify and gather metrics and data that will be needed to answer those questions. These are referred to as metrics.

6.2 CSFs and KPIs

Before we go further on the topic of measurements and metrics, we need to define a few terms:

- **Critical success factors** (CSFs) These are things that must happen for the achievement of organizational goals and objectives. It is important to prioritize CSFs and focus on the top two or three for each process.

---

3 Cameron, W. B. (1963). *Informal Sociology: A Casual Introduction to Sociological Thinking*. Random House, New York.
4 Cabinet Office (2011). *ITIL Continual Service Improvement*. The Stationery Office, London.

- **Key performance indicators** (KPIs) These are indicators (information) that will assist an organization in assessing its performance and effectiveness in achieving stated goals and objectives (CSFs). They:
    - Measure progress towards the achievement of your CSFs
    - Reflect key process aspects such as quality, performance, value and compliance
    - Can be either qualitative (survey comments) or quantitative (numerical)
    - Identify areas where improvements are needed.

    It is important to rank KPIs and focus on the top two or three for each CSF.

- **Metric** This is a measure of an organization's activities and performance as it relates to the management of a process or activity. Metrics can be people related, process related, service related or technology related.

- **Baseline** This represents a marker, or starting point, for later comparison. Baselines are used to establish an initial data point in order to measure changes in performance or the effect of process improvements over time. Without establishing a baseline, it can be difficult to calculate and communicate measured improvements.

6.2.1 Common CSFs and KPIs

Each organization will need to determine its vision, goals and objectives for problem management and then, based upon those, identify the CSFs, supporting KPIs, metrics and measurements that are meaningful to the organization. We advise no more than three CSFs per process and no more than three KPIs per CSF. Table 6.1 provides an example of common CSFs and KPIs for problem management.

Table 6.1 Common CSFs and KPIs for problem management

Critical success factors	Key performance indicators
1 Improve service quality	(a) Reduction in the number of incidents (over time) affecting services to customers
	(b) Increased percentage of proactive versus reactive changes submitted by problem management
2 Minimize impact of problems	(a) Reduction in average time to implement fixes to problems
	(b) Increase in first-call resolution through use of workarounds
3 Resolve problems effectively and efficiently	(a) Reduction in the backlog of open problems
	(b) Increase in the number of problems resolved within their target resolution times

The following are comments and clarifications regarding the KPIs listed in Table 6.1.

1(a) This KPI should be reported by each technical support group, or technology domain. If your infrastructure technology, your customer base and the services you provide remain constant, then over a period of time you should see a reduction in the total number of incidents reported because you are permanently fixing recurring incidents. Additionally, your proactive problem management activities should be preventing incidents from occurring in the first place. You will want to report for each technology domain because that gives you indications as to which technical support groups are performing problem management activities and improving the infrastructure for which they are responsible.

1(b) This KPI helps to quantify the effectiveness of proactive problem management. To measure this, you will need a way to identify problem records that were opened proactively as opposed to reactively. This could be a simple indicator stored on the problem record or built into the categorization scheme for problems.

2(a) This KPI provides an indication as to whether you are improving (getting faster at) your ability and capabilities to identify and implement permanent fixes.

2(b) This KPI validates that workarounds are being recorded and that incident matching is being performed.

3(a) Tracking and reporting on this KPI can tell you at both an IT organizational level and by technical support group whether problems are being progressed to known errors and whether known errors are being removed through permanent fixes.

3(b) This KPI assumes that you have set target resolution times for problem records. This is an organizational decision which we discussed back in Chapter 3.

6.2.2 Additional CSFs for problem management

Examples of additional problem management CSFs include:

- Increase the use of the problem management process
- Produce actionable problem management reports
- Provide sufficient training for IT staff performing problem management tasks
- Acquire, configure and implement supporting tools for the problem management process
- Demonstrate management support and commitment to problem management.

6.2.3 Additional KPIs for problem management

Now that you have some good ideas for CSFs, Table 6.2 provides some examples of typical problem management KPIs to consider.

Table 6.2 Additional KPIs to consider for problem management

KPIs	Description/explanation
The total number of problems recorded during the reporting period	Number of problems opened during the reporting period. There should be an increase initially as an organization implements problem management, but later this will decrease as problem resolution capabilities mature
The total number of known errors (or knowledge articles) created during the reporting period	Number of known error records created during the reporting period. There should be an increase initially as an organization implements problem management. This demonstrates that root causes and workarounds are being identified
The number and percentage of problems or known errors that missed their target resolution goals	The number of problems and known errors that were not resolved within the defined resolution targets, based on the priority of the record. This metric should trend downwards over time as problem resolution capabilities mature
Number of requests for change (RFCs) submitted from problem management	Number of RFCs submitted to permanently remove errors from the environment. This demonstrates that permanent fixes are being identified and implemented
Elapsed time on resolved problems	The total elapsed time on resolved problems, based on the priority of the record (i.e. how long did it take from open to resolved?)
Elapsed time on outstanding problems	The elapsed time to date on outstanding problems, based on the priority of the record (i.e. how long have they been open?). This is sometimes referred to as an aging report

Targets should be set for each KPI so that actual performance can be measured towards the goal. KPI reports can be 'snapshot reports' (for a specific point in time), as well as 'trending reports', which are used to show progress towards your stated goals and objectives. For example, as your problem management capabilities mature over time, you should see a reduction in elapsed time and resources required to resolve problems by the technical teams. At some point, however, this reduction in time and resources will level out once the less complex problems are solved.

6.3 Management reporting

The process owner is responsible for identifying the informational requirements and reporting that stakeholders and customers need from the problem management process. This includes determining the frequency of the reporting and the format(s) with which these reports are to be delivered. Identifying reporting requirements will help to ensure that the reports are targeted and actionable.

Problem Management

> **Note**
> Reporting needs will evolve over time as the process becomes more mature. And, remember, reports will only be as accurate as the source data being used.

Typical report recipient groups include:

- Customers and users
- Service partners
- Service owners
- Suppliers
- Process owners and process managers
- Functional managers
- IT staff
- Executive management.

Creating and producing the necessary reports is the role of the report specialist. The report specialist may produce standard reports and queries or ad hoc reports for stakeholders using the ITSM tool, reporting tools and supporting databases.

Problem management reports are often associated with one of the following three categories:

- Strategic level (process efficiency and effectiveness reports)
- Tactical level (root cause analysis, verification and audit reports)
- Operational level (informational, trending and compliance reports).

To attain a clear understanding of the nature of incidents and problems and their impact on the business, data should be analysed from multiple perspectives (e.g. by problem category, priority, technical support group, assignee, location, status, business unit impact and duration). Face-to-face meetings to review the reports should occur regularly between the process manager and process owner, technical support groups, problem assignees, IT management and key stakeholders. These meetings can be used to confirm process compliance, that stakeholder needs are met, and for the identification of continual improvement opportunities.

A word of caution – IT departments frequently produce copious reports and push them to a wide audience. When this happens, some recipients get so overwhelmed with reports that they cease looking at them, while others often don't know what the report is telling them, or what they should do with it. It is important to be focused on what you report and to whom you provide the information. It is frequently helpful to advise recipients on what actions to take based on the information they're looking at. At the very least, recipients should be taught how to use reports as action item identifiers.

Once the reports are designed, the production of the reports should occur on a scheduled basis and they should be made available to recipients through various formats such as the intranet, SharePoint sites, automated emails and reporting tools. A report catalogue can be used to identify what reports are being created, for whom, their frequency and their delivery method. Table 6.3 provides an example of a report catalogue for problem management.

In summary, when you've agreed with key stakeholders what to measure and report on for problem management, ask yourself these questions:

- What is important to be measured, and are we measuring it?
- Do the identified metrics align with the underlying goals of the business?
- Are the reports actionable and do they have targeted audiences?
- Will the reports create value by providing information that has a positive effect on decisions and behaviour?
- What is the value of the reports versus the cost or difficulty of producing them?

6.4 Process maturity assessments

Another way of measuring your organization's progress towards achieving its process goals and objectives is to perform a process maturity assessment.

We spoke earlier of establishing a baseline – a marker, or starting point, for later comparison. A process maturity assessment is used to establish a process baseline (current state) to measure the effect of process improvements over time (future state). After establishing your vision for problem management, the process maturity assessment helps determine where you are today in relation to that vision.

There are several process maturity assessment tools available in the market. Some of the more commonly known assessments are Carnegie Mellon University's CMMI (Capability Maturity Model Integration)[5] and the International Organization for Standardization ISO/IEC 33001:2015.[6] The assessments ask a number of questions to evaluate an organization's current process capabilities and where improvements in process capabilities are needed, based on ITSM frameworks and industry best practices. Many of these assessments use a scale of 0 to 5 or 1 to 5, often in half-point increments (higher numbers representing higher maturity levels) to measure an organization's process maturity level.

---

5   CMMI is an industry-accepted process improvement model developed by Carnegie Mellon University for the purpose of helping organizations appraise the maturity of their processes.

6   ISO/IEC 33001:2015 is an international standard for evaluating the maturity of processes for technology organizations.

Table 6.3 Example of common problem management reports

Report title	Description	Purpose	Frequency	Recipients	Actions to take	Delivery methods
Opened problem/ known error report (for the reporting period) reported by: 1. Support group 2. Priority 3. Status 4. Affected service 5. Problem category	A report that shows how many problems and known errors were opened, who they were assigned to and their priority	To identify if problems are being opened appropriately; to determine if problems are being progressed to known errors; and to identify which support groups are performing problem management activities and what their current problem workload is	Weekly Monthly trending	First-line IT management Incident manager Problem manager ITSM director	Ensure problem records are being opened appropriately Ensure problem records are being assigned in a timely manner Ensure problem records are being assigned to appropriately skilled individuals to ensure progress towards permanent solution Look for multiple records with the same affected service and use this information to help set priorities	Dashboard Report Query
Unresolved problem/ known error report reported by: 1. Support group 2. Priority 3. Status 4. Duration 5. Affected service 6. Problem category	A report that provides a total count of all open problem and known error records and how long they have been open	To determine how successful we are at solving problems; to identify the age of open problem/ known error records	Weekly Monthly trending	All IT management Problem manager ITSM director	Ensure 'pending' records are being worked on, paying special attention to records with a 'pending vendor' status Ensure problems are being progressed to known errors and permanent solutions (i.e. status = 'pending change') Determine which support groups are taking the most time to resolve problems and why, and take corrective action	Dashboard Report Query

Mean time to resolve report reported by: 1. Support group 2. Priority 3. Affected service 4. Problem category 5. Root cause 6. Elapsed time	This report[a] shows the mean elapsed time to implementation of problem solutions by priority and support group	To determine how efficiently we are permanently solving problems. Elapsed time should trend downwards over time	Monthly Year-to-date trending	All IT management Problem manager ITSM director IT staff	Determine which support groups take the most time to solve problems and determine why Implement improvements and corrective actions, as necessary	Dashboard Report Bulletin board
Problem/known error to RFC report (for the reporting period) reported by: 1. Support group 2. Priority 3. Status 4. Affected service 5. Problem category (Status = pending change)	Shows how many fixes have been submitted for implementation approval to permanently remove an error from the infrastructure	To track approvals through the change management process for open problems and known errors	Weekly	IT management Problem manager Change manager	Determine the status of the RFC within the change management process Escalate the priority of the change record, if necessary, to get the fix expedited	Report Query
Record status update report reported by: 1. Support group 2. Priority 3. Assignee	Shows whether the support groups are updating problem records with new information according to the parameters defined in the standard operating procedure	To determine if timely information is being provided to the service desk in the problem records and to determine compliance with the process	Weekly Monthly	IT management Problem manager	Ensure problem and known error records are being updated to reflect current status and new information Determine which support groups are not complying with process directives and why, and take corrective action	Report

Table continues

Table 6.3 continued

Report title	Description	Purpose	Frequency	Recipients	Actions to take	Delivery methods
Top 10 report reported by: 1. Problem category 2. Status 3. Priority 4. No. of linked incident records 5. Support group 6. Assignee	Shows the problems that have the greatest potential for impacting services	To understand the business impact of problems and evaluate resources assigned	Daily Weekly	IT management Problem manager Service desk	Determine if enough and appropriately skilled staff are assigned to these highly visible problems Engage additional skilled resources and escalate actions as necessary	Dashboard Report Query

a The report should be categorized by the support group and sent to the senior IT manager.

> **Note**
> It is often advantageous to hire a third-party assessing organization to perform the process maturity assessment rather than performing a self-assessment, as it is difficult for IT organizations to be objective when evaluating their process capabilities. It is the goal of these third-party assessments to turn the assessment findings into an understandable, impartial and actionable set of recommendations and next steps (roadmap) for process improvement.

The following are major topics and questions that should be considered when assessing the maturity of your process and planning for your future state.

6.4.1 Process
- To what degree is the organization committed to a process-based approach?
- Are the benefits of a process approach understood?
- Is the process approach supported?
- Do the processes successfully integrate technology silos?
- Is there evidence of people not taking expected ownership and/or responsibility?

6.4.2 People
- Are people working effectively together in teams?
- Are roles clearly defined for authority and responsibility?
- Are effective communication structures in place?
- Are effective meeting practices in place?
- Are effective training plans in place?

6.4.3 Culture
- Are people focused on the needs of the customer/organization?
- Do managers demonstrate effective leadership skills in support of change?
- How willing/able is the organization to accept change (new ways of thinking and acting)?
- Do people view change with scepticism?
- Are people involved and committed when changes are introduced?
- Do people follow procedures?
- Are there consequences if procedures aren't followed?
- What is the level of employee satisfaction?

6.4.4 Tools

- What ITSM tools are in use?
- Are the tools enabling the service management processes?
- Are the tools integrated (data and workflow)?
- Do the tools meet current and future needs?
- Are the tools easily configurable?

6.4.5 Process improvement project plan

Before a process improvement plan can be developed, a decision regarding the future target level for process maturity needs to be made. You've determined your vision and you know what your current state is, but where do you need to be from both the business and IT perspective? Questions to consider when determining the target level of maturity are:

- Do the IT service provider and the organization share the same view of the role, quality and maturity of IT?
- What do the organization's stakeholders need from IT?
- What maturity level does the organization expect of IT?
- What is the benefit versus the cost and risk of achieving this level of maturity?

Once there is organizational agreement on the desired target maturity level, it's time to develop your process implementation or improvement plan. You will need to determine the actions required (How do we get there?) to achieve the desired maturity level and then create a project plan and charter with key stakeholders that will guide you to that next level of maturity.

Organizations planning to adopt and implement a successful and effective problem management process should consider the following when building their project plan:

- Communicate the need for problem management
- Create a clear process vision and mission
- Establish steadfast sponsorship
- Ensure organizational participation in the design and implementation
- Use a disciplined project management approach
- Address organizational change management (the people side of change)
- Identify the functional and technical requirements needed to support the plan's objectives
- Identify training and support requirements.

Appendix G provides an example of a project plan for implementing or improving a process. It can be tailored to the individual needs and culture of your organization.

6.4.6 Communication

Developing an effective communication plan or campaign is very important to the success of the project. This will help to ensure that stakeholders are kept informed through the use of consistent messaging methods, timetables and technologies, with the goal of strengthening understanding and commitment to the project. For each stakeholder group, the question 'What's in it for me?' (WIIFM) should be answered.

Communication plans should identify what messages need to be communicated, to whom, who the content owner is, delivery methods, frequency of the communication, review and publication date deadlines. Appendix H provides a template to assist in developing your communication plan. The 'message/goal' column should tie back to tasks identified in your project plan.

There are several different delivery methods that can be used for communicating key messages. These may include use of:

- Brochures
- Conference calls
- Corporate newsletters
- Email
- Intranets
- Posters
- SharePoint sites
- Social media
- Staff meetings
- Training sessions.

Once your process improvement plan has been implemented, how will you know if you have achieved the goals that you have set for yourselves? Perform another process maturity assessment and look to your metrics and measurements for verification!

7 Keys to success

By now you have probably been thinking, 'What are the success factors I need to consider for implementing problem management effectively in my organization? How do I convey the value of problem management to my organization? How will I manage the organizational change aspects of implementing problem management?'

7.1 Common success factors

There are seven common success areas to be considered when implementing problem management in any organization. Those categories are:

- Vision and leadership
- Process
- People
- Technology and data
- Communications
- Reporting
- Training.

7.1.1 Vision and leadership

- Establish your vision, purpose and scope for implementing a formal problem management process. Without the establishment and consistent communication of a sound vision and purpose, it will be nearly impossible to gain commitment from the staff and key stakeholders in support of this undertaking. A clear and common set of objectives linked to the vision must be developed, communicated and shared across the organization.

- Identify a problem management process 'champion'. The process champion should be an influential leader within the organization who has credibility for getting the right things done and who will be able to help communicate and sell the problem management vision to the business and IT. This person should be able to obtain senior leadership support (both business and IT) for the design and implementation of the process.

- Identify and quantify the return on investment (not solely monetary) for performing problem management activities. This return on investment will need to be clearly documented and communicated. We will talk more about this later in this chapter.

7.1.2 Process

- An effective incident management process must exist that logs all incidents and records complete, accurate and valid data.
- All problems should be identified, logged, monitored and controlled from open to close.
- A problem management process policy supported by process plans and procedures must be defined, documented and accessible to staff. Key components of the process design should include:
    - Clear criteria for the identification and definition of a problem
    - Clear definitions and consistent use of key terms throughout the process
    - Consistent use of standardized methods for the handling of problems that are aligned with business objectives and tied back to service level agreements
    - Shared categorization and prioritization schemes between incident and problem management
    - Accurate categorization and assignment of problems to the appropriate support group in order to expedite the investigation, diagnosis and development of a permanent solution
    - Appropriate assignment of problem priority
    - The linking of reactive problem records to the incidents that triggered them and to the CIs that are impacted
    - Establishment of clear criteria for the successful resolution and restoration of service, as well as for closing a problem record
    - Defined responsibility for the completeness and accuracy of the data.
- Problem management must be integrated with other key ITSM processes, including:
    - Incident management
    - Change management
    - Release management
    - Configuration management
    - Capacity management
    - Service level management.
- Proactive problem management activities must be performed and measured. This includes the trending of incidents with an enterprise-wide view and the auditing of infrastructure.

- Accurate and meaningful reporting must be available to stakeholders and to the other service management processes.
- Problem management reviews must be consistently performed for lessons learned and continual process improvement. Attention should be given to workflow, tools used, staff assignments, quality of data captured, performance and compliance by various technical support groups, and to whether process goals and objectives are being achieved.
- Process shortcomings (tasks, procedures, communication, training, collaboration, missed service level targets etc.) must be reported to the process owner for improvement and correction.

7.1.3 People

- Executive sponsorship is essential. Leadership should be engaged in consistent communication of the benefits of the process, and involved in escalated issues concerning enforcement of the process.
- Define and assign roles, responsibilities and ownership of problems.
- Fill roles with sufficiently trained and responsible people.
- Allocate a sufficient number of staff to perform problem management activities, ensuring they have enough time to perform such activities.
- Ensure that root cause analysis is performed by appropriately skilled and trained staff.
- Require support group members, service partners, suppliers and other stakeholders to comply with the problem management process.
- Identify a technical support group to pilot the new or improved process and the supporting technology. We can't overemphasize the importance of this statement. We have seen this strategy work effectively time and again. IT organizations do not always design and implement an effective problem management process the first time. Thus, identifying a technical support group that is willing, or even excited, about performing problem management activities and testing the process is critical to the process roll-out and adoption by the organization. The pilot team provides feedback on the process to help put in place any adjustments needed before the process is further implemented. Additionally, pilot team members are able to act as mentors to other technical support groups as the process is subsequently rolled out.

7.1.4 Technology and data

- Having a robust, integrated suite of enterprise-wide tools that enables the storage and accessibility of data, information and knowledge is critical for the problem management process. However, the process should be properly defined and designed before you start looking at technology. Automating a bad process just means that you 'get faster at doing it incorrectly'. Until you understand the process, its data requirements and how it will be implemented in your organization, you are not ready to start shopping for tools. We often hear of organizations that purchase an ITSM tool and then proceed to design their processes based on the limitations of the tool. These actions are backwards.

- Problem management process requirements should be an important consideration when selecting an ITSM tool. When looking for tools, you should focus on those tools that support the entire lifecycle of the problem: the creation of a problem record and capturing its associated data; tracking the problem record status; setting root cause and resolution codes; and reassignment and escalation of the problem.
- There are a number of aspects to consider when making your tool selection. The tool should:
  - Use commonly accepted ITSM terms and definitions
  - Support the designed process workflow
  - Support a knowledge base where data is captured, maintained and accessible for use by support personnel and/or end-users
  - Integrate effectively with other processes such as incident, change and configuration management
  - Provide comprehensive search, data mining and reporting capabilities, enabling sharing of information and accurate analysis for informed decision-making
  - Enable the capture of service achievement data and metrics, and provide support for a variety of reporting distribution methods
  - Support the implementation of access controls to data and records based on defined process roles
  - Provide automation that supports and assists in enforcing process rules, relationships between records, and notifications to problem analysts and stakeholders.
- In addition to the above list of considerations, there are a number of other questions you should ask when assessing process-supporting tools:
  - Is the tool easy to configure and tailor to match and support your designed process?
  - What is the cost of maintaining the tool?
  - Does the tool provide an historical activity log for the problem?
  - Does the tool allow problem assignment by category, service, or configuration item type?
  - Does the tool allow the creation of a change record from a problem record and automatically link the two?

- How and where does the tool allow for storage of the temporary workaround – i.e. how are known errors entered, stored, accessed and searched by both support group personnel and end-users?
- How does the tool document and manage knowledge articles pertaining to problems and known errors?
- Does the tool support predefined routing and notification schemes to technical support groups and key stakeholders?
- Can multiple incidents with similar symptoms be linked to a parent incident record, and that parent incident record be linked to a problem or known error record?
- How are problem record status changes handled by the tool? Can a resolved or closed problem record be reopened and rolled back to a previous status?
- Can an existing problem record be cloned for a similar but different problem record, to minimize data entry?
- What real-time trending and querying capabilities does the tool have?
- What graphical display capabilities of data and information does the tool have?
- Does the tool have the ability to differentiate between reactive and proactive problem records?
- What capability does the tool have to interface with other enterprise tools (e.g. event monitoring tools, notification tools) or third-party systems?

7.1.5 Communications

- There should be ongoing communication from executive sponsors to reinforce the problem process vision, purpose, principles, focus and value to the business.
- Process benefits and achievements should be consistently communicated to all process support staff and key stakeholders.
- The importance of complying with the process and the performance of process activities should continually be reinforced.
- Information and knowledge sharing, communication and collaboration among the technical support groups should be strongly encouraged and monitored.
- Meetings with key stakeholders and suppliers where problem management concerns and activities are discussed should be held regularly.
- Information exchanges between problem management and service level management regarding the potential impact on service level agreements and organizational performance should occur on a regular basis.

7.1.6 Reporting

- Process reporting requirements and the identification of report recipients should be determined by the process owner.
- Reporting should be focused on organizational needs that are based on clear goals and objectives.
- The identified reports should be aligned with service level requirements.
- Clearly defined metrics that are of value and that reflect process performance, compliance and benefits, and that are aligned with key performance indicators and critical success factors, should be used to measure the process.
- The data source for each metric must be identified and its completeness and accuracy verified.
- Delivery of accurate and meaningful reports to individuals and key stakeholders should occur on an agreed and pre-scheduled basis.

7.1.7 Training

To ensure success of the process and to prepare individuals to successfully perform problem management activities, all participants in the problem management process should be trained based on their role within the process. Key training success factors include:

- Identifying key participants and their role within the process, assessing their current skills and competencies, and then scheduling them for training
- Creating training materials specific to the different roles identified within the process
- Designing, developing and delivering 'how to' guides
- Delivering just-in-time training appropriate to the implementation and roll-out of the process
- Allowing access to the problem management tool (or module) only after successful completion of problem management training has been verified
- Ensuring that you have ongoing process education and training for all process participants, especially new employees
- Ensuring timely training updates when changes have been made to the process.

Table 7.1 provides an example of training mapped to roles within the problem management process. The column headings are explained in the table footnotes.

In addition to process-related training, consideration should be given to other types of 'soft skill' training that may be required, based upon the role of the individual. Examples include training for the development of the following skills:

Keys to success

- Customer service
- Negotiation and consensus building
- Conflict resolution
- Oral and written communication
- Resource management and team building.

Table 7.1 Process training mapped to process roles

Role	High-level process training[a]	Detailed process training[b]	ITSM tool training[c]	Root cause analysis techniques training[d]	Service restoration training – intermediate level[e]
Process owner	X	X			X
Problem manager	X	X	X	X	X
Support groups	X	X	X	X	
IT managers	X				
Incident manager	X	X	X		X
Knowledge manager	X		X		
Service desk manager	X		X		X
Service desk agent	X		X		
Change manager	X				
Report specialist	X		X		

a Training consists of roles and responsibilities, process flow (high level), process relationships, metrics and reporting, and general ITSM tool usage.

b Training includes detailed process activities, tasks and workflow training.

c (Specific to problem management) Training includes detailed ITSM tool training and report generation. Dependent on specific roles, training may also include how to link incident records to problem records, problem records to known errors and knowledge base articles, and problem records to change records.

d In-depth industry training on one or more root cause analysis techniques (e.g. Kepner–Tregoe, fault tree analysis etc.).

e An intermediate level of training in service restoration that covers both incident and problem management.

129

7.1.8 Common pitfalls to avoid

No discussion on success factors for implementing problem management would be complete without mentioning some common pitfalls that organizations encounter:

- Focusing too much on technology instead of organizational goals
- Failing to incorporate proactive problem management into the overall process
- Trying to investigate and diagnose every problem
- Failing to implement the identified solutions
- Having ineffective interfaces between incident, problem, change and configuration management
- Having inadequate and/or poor-quality data captured in the incident management process
- Failure to allocate staff time for problem management activities
- Failure to focus on the problems that cause 80% of the service disruptions
- Having ineffective or no leadership and management commitment in support of the process
- Failure to reward individuals and teams for successfully performing problem management activities.

7.2 Selling problem management – developing your business case

The word 'selling' can often have a negative connotation. It can imply that we are pushing something to people that they don't really need or want, sometimes through the use of deceptive or manipulative practices. That is certainly not what we are suggesting here. Our use of the word 'selling' is in the context of articulating the benefits and value of implementing a formal problem management process. It is about developing the business case for problem management and getting 'buy-in'. While the need to invest in customer-facing, business-impacting processes such as incident management and request fulfilment is usually easy to justify, the true value of problem management may not initially be as obvious to the business.

Fire-fighting and fire prevention

Organizations often use the term 'fire-fighting', but as a fire chief reminds us, 'Our fire department has two roles, fire-fighting and fire prevention – we must be good at both!' For many organizations, the initial value of problem management will be fire-fighting, where problem management is involved in the development of knowledge articles and workarounds so that incidents can be quickly resolved. As the problem management process matures, organizations will shift resources to fire prevention; providing highly reliable services as a result of identifying and fixing potential problems before they impact users. Just as with the fire department, the true value of problem management comes from the proper balance of reactive and proactive activities.

7.2.1 Selling problem management to the organization

We stated earlier that gaining approval for the investment in problem management starts with creating your vision and communicating a sense of urgency around that vision. In efforts to promote and communicate your vision, you need to be able to answer the following questions:

- What is it we need to accomplish?
- What pain points need to be addressed?
- What problems need to be solved?
- Who will be involved?
- Who will be affected?
- What is the planned timescale?
- What are the constraints?
- What are the benefits, both tangible and intangible?

In Chapter 1, we listed the benefits of implementing a formal and sound problem management process. These include having a standard approach to problem management, higher levels of compliance with service level agreements, increased customer satisfaction with IT and improved service quality. While these are indeed, along with others, outcomes and benefits of problem management, many would say these are soft benefits whose value is difficult to quantify.

An organization's investment of time, money and resources in problem management will be weighed against the benefits derived from the investment of these same resources in other potential organizational endeavours. Thus, the problem management vision, objectives and goals have to be tied back to your company's business objectives and drivers. Aligning IT investments back to business objectives and providing evidence that this investment helps the business achieve its objectives will go a long way in gaining approval for an investment in problem management. Your focus must be on the achievement of business outcomes.

We should first ask, 'What is important to the business?' One way to determine that is to read your company's annual report and your company's strategic goals and objectives. Is it to reduce costs, increase speed to delivery, reduce customer complaints, improve resource use, or improve the quality of your products? Problem management benefits are real. You need to be able to articulate to the decision-makers the value of their investment in business terms: revenue growth, income growth, protecting future revenues, customer retention, future cost avoidance or regulatory compliance. This is where a business case comes into play.

7.2.2 Developing a business case

The business case provides justification for the expenditure of organizational resources based on expected benefits and the financial return on investment (ROI). The actual format and content of a business case varies from one organization to another. The following is a simplified structure for a business case.

- Executive summary (problem statement, goals, objectives, recommended approach)
- Introduction (background, business needs and desired outcomes)
- Assumptions
- Business risks and impacts (financial and non-financial)
- Viable options considered (be sure to include the option of taking no action):
  - Option 1 (description, rationale, benefits, ROI analysis)
  - Option 2 (description, rationale, benefits, ROI analysis)
  - Option 3 (description, rationale, benefits, ROI analysis)
- Recommendations and conclusions.

7.2.2.1 Return on investment

ROI is a financial term used to measure the percentage return on an investment, usually over a period of time. It is often used to compare different investment choices. To calculate ROI, the benefits (return) of an investment are divided by the cost of the investment. The formula looks like the following:

$$ROI = Return/Costs \times 100\%$$

Costs are start-up costs plus any ongoing annual costs. Return is savings over the defined period (often 3–5 years) after costs have been subtracted. Costs and returns should be in the same currency.

ROI is expressed as a percentage. An investment should not be undertaken if the ROI is negative, or if there are other investment choices with a higher ROI.

Below we give two example calculations for ROI.

ROI based on reducing service restoration time (reactive problem management) – fire-fighting
What would the financial benefits be to the business if you were able to reduce the time it takes to resolve an incident through the use of knowledge articles and workarounds provided by problem management? While there would clearly be business productivity savings for the users who are impacted, in the following calculation we will determine the potential savings in IT support costs. Note that the numbers in the following example are fictitious and were chosen to simplify the calculations involved in determining ROI.

Current state assumptions:

- 60 minutes (1 hour) – average time to resolve an incident
- £25 per hour – average IT support team hourly rate
- 12,000 – Number of incidents annually
- £300,000 – annual cost of incident management (£25 × 1 hour × 12,000 incidents = £300,000).

Future state assumptions:

- 6 minutes (0.1 hour) – average time to resolve an incident using knowledge articles provided by problem management
- £25 per hour – average IT support team hourly rate
- 12,000 – number of incidents annually
- £30,000 – annual cost of incident management (£25 × 0.1 hour × 12,000 incidents = £30,000).

Annual IT support savings:

- £270,000 – annual savings (£300,000 current state – £30,000 future state).

Problem management project cost assumptions (one-time costs):

- £40,000 – problem management process design workshop sessions
- £10,000 – knowledge management training for 10 staff
- £25,000 – ITSM tool enhancements.

Ongoing problem management cost assumptions (annual):

- £50,000 – dedicated staffing to develop and publish workarounds and knowledge articles.

Total first-year cost:

- £125,000 = (£40,000 workshops + £10,000 knowledge management training + £25,000 tools + £50,000 staff).

Year 1 ROI = 116%. ROI = (Return £270,000 – Costs £125,000)/Costs £125,000 × 100%

3-year ROI = 260%. ROI = (Return £270,000 × 3 years) – (Costs £125,000 year 1 + £50,000 year 2 + £50,000 year 3)/(Costs £125,000 year 1 + £50,000 year 2 + £50,000 year 3) × 100%

As you can see from the example above, after the one-time (initial) costs were recovered, the savings in subsequent years are even more impressive!

ROI based on increased business productivity (proactive problem management) – fire prevention

Another consideration when quantifying the financial benefits of problem management is reduction in business downtime costs. When services are unavailable there are several different types of costs associated with that downtime:

- Lost end-user productivity
- Opportunity costs from slipped projects
- Lost revenue from lost sales
- Penalties for missed service level targets
- Damage to the company reputation.

Let's choose one of these to investigate further. Lost end-user productivity could be a result of an unstable infrastructure. Repeat incidents are a regular occurrence because problem management is not investigating and permanently resolving incidents. Of course, some companies will have fewer outages but for longer duration, while others will have more frequent outages of shorter duration. The number of users affected will also vary significantly between companies. Note that the numbers in the following example are fictitious and were chosen to simplify the calculations involved in determining ROI.

Current state assumptions:

- 4 hours – average time to restore a business service outage
- £40 per hour – average salary for business staff
- 50 users – number of business staff impacted by a typical outage
- 52 outages per year – 1 outage per week
- £416,000 – annual lost productivity (4 hours × £40 per hour × 50 users × 52 outages per year).

Future state assumptions:

- 4 hours – average time to restore a business service outage
- £40 per hour – average salary for business staff
- 50 users – number of business staff impacted by a typical outage
- 2 outages per year
- £16,000 – annual lost productivity (4 hours × £40 per hour × 50 users × 2 outages per year).

Annual business productivity savings:

- £400,000 annual savings (£416,000 current state – £16,000 future state).

Problem management project cost assumptions (one-time costs):

- £40,000 – problem management process design workshop sessions
- £10,000 – root cause analysis (RCA) training for 10 staff
- £25,000 – ITSM tool enhancements.

Ongoing problem management cost assumptions (annual):

- £50,000 – dedicated staffing for proactive problem management (fix it before it breaks).

Total first-year cost:

- £125,000 = (£40,000 workshops + £10,000 RCA training + £25,000 tools + £50,000 staff).

Year 1 ROI = 220%. ROI = (Return £400,000 – Costs £125,000)/Costs £125,000 × 100%

3-year ROI = 433%. ROI = (Return £400,000 × 3 years) – (Costs £125,000 year 1 + £50,000 year 2 + £50,000 year 3)/(Costs £125,000 year 1 + £50,000 year 2 + £50,000 year 3) × 100%

ROI summary

We don't want you to come to the end of this section and believe that the ROI examples we have provided are representative of a typical organization. In fact, the examples are there only to show how ROI is calculated and to get you thinking about how you can incorporate both reactive and proactive savings into your business case for investing in problem management.

7.2.3 Final thoughts on the value of problem management

Other strategies for promoting and selling problem management within your organization should include using data from credible industry research firms and outside experts, and networking with other companies who have benefited from the implementation of problem management.

7.3 Addressing organizational change

Whether you are improving an existing problem management process or implementing one for the first time, you must address and manage organizational change. Organizational change management is a set of activities designed to manage change effectively in order to minimize risk and disruption to staff and services.

People react to change in different ways. When maturing internal processes, an organization will need to move from an informal, relationship-based organization, to one that is a formal,

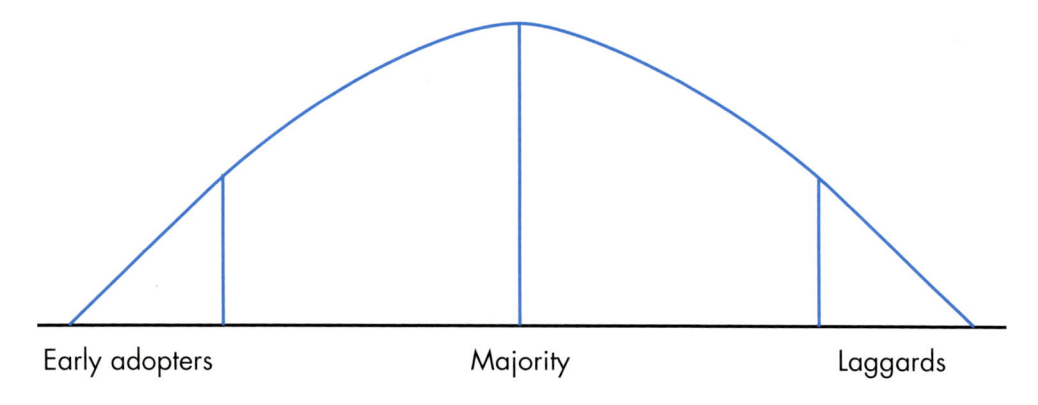

Figure 7.1 Adopter categorization

rules-based organization. You may be moving from a 'we have no process' position, to enforcing a standardized and documented process. Some people are going to be accepting of the change; others will resist.

It is generally agreed that there is a distribution curve for acceptance of change, as shown in Figure 7.1. The terminology is as follows:

- **Early adopters** These are the people who are going to be excited about the change. They clearly see the need for it; they are fully behind it; they are 'gung ho' about it; they wonder what took you so long; they want to be a part of the change and offer their assistance.
- **Laggards** These are the people who won't like it. They don't like change of any kind. They are the 'Eeyores'[7] of your organization. You know who they are. They don't get it; they don't want to get it; they will never get it; and they will do what they can to keep it from succeeding.
- **Majority** These are the people who 'sit on the fence' watching to see which way the wind blows. They are not supportive, and yet they are not resistant to the change. They sit back with a cautious eye, watching the lie of the land to see which way the battle will go before they take sides.

The following are some potential adoption strategies to consider:

- 'Seed' the majority with early adopters (positive change agents).
- Keep the laggards away from the majority (we don't want the majority to be negatively influenced).

---

7 Eeyore is a character in the Winnie-the-Pooh books by A. A. Milne. He is generally pessimistic and gloomy.

- Include laggards in the process design or improvement project. Choose laggards that you feel you can win over through their participation and influence in the process design or improvement project. If you can win them over, they often become the best positive change agents and will play a large role in winning others.
- Tie problem management activities and successes to each employee's annual merit compensation. This will reward the early adopters, while serving as an incentive for the majority and laggards to embrace the change.

It is important to acknowledge that there are different (up and down) phases of emotion and reaction that people go through when facing change. Be patient and proactive. Anticipate and mitigate the predictable negative reaction to change. Recognize and support staff as they go through different phases. The downward phases often end in doubt and distrust of actions or decisions, no matter what the context. It often takes time before individuals begin their upward phases; moving from experimentation to reluctance, then to confidence and eventually to acceptance. These emotional phases are represented in Figure 7.2.

7.4 Final thoughts

We left addressing organizational change to the last, because this may be the most difficult challenge to overcome. Be diligent about developing awareness, communication, education, training and recognition campaigns to help overcome this challenge. Involve more staff in the decision-making of the new or improved process to help ensure constructive adoption.

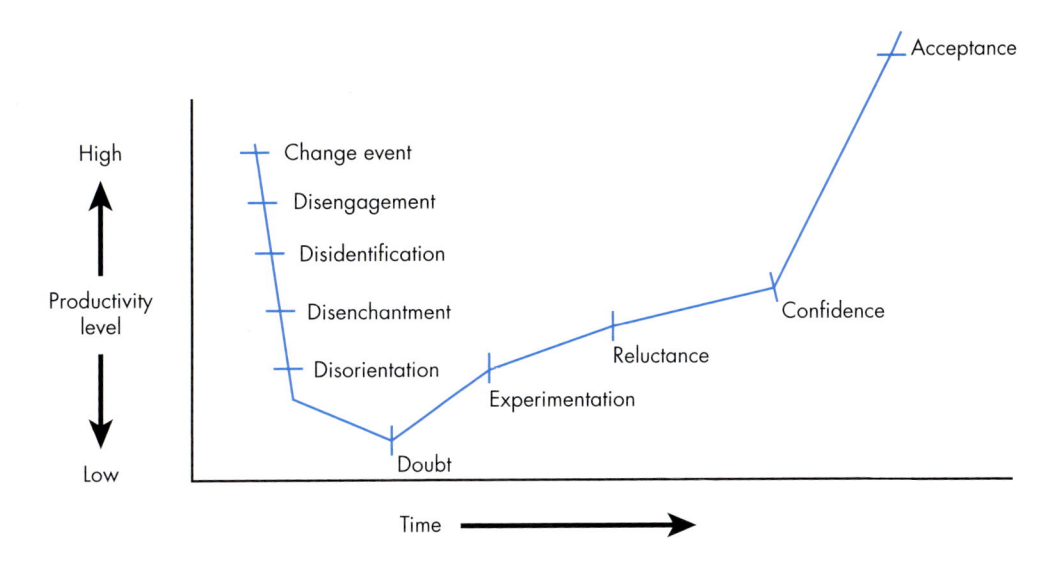

Figure 7.2 Reactions to organizational change

Based on the transition model developed by William Bridges in *Transitions: Making Sense of Life's Changes* (Da Capo Press, 2004)

Be sure to set realistic timelines and clear deliverables. Don't expect major benefits too soon. This can be a long-term initiative, so use project management discipline and prioritize your deliverables in phases.

Remember that this is a journey, not a destination. You can rest assured that you are not alone in your journey. Other IT organizations have successfully made this important journey. Identify and network with these organizations, or local interest groups, and use elements of their experiences to help you identify and refine your approach to successful problem management implementation.

Don't let perfect get in the way of good! Come back to this publication often, to the practical principles contained within it, and reapply as necessary.

We wish you the very best on your problem management journey.

As we close this chapter and the publication, we leave you with a summary listing of keys to your problem management implementation success:

- Show progress early – people need to see the benefits
- Prepare the organization for a culture change and promote the right culture
- Be business, service and customer focused
- Promote organizational discipline
- Use quick wins to achieve and sustain momentum
- Use wins to leverage more wins
- Make sure employees understand the benefits to the organization, and to themselves
- Provide recognition and motivation
- Demonstrate progress towards targets and business objectives
- Facilitate changes in action plans to ensure objectives are accomplished
- Describe setbacks and what is being done to get back on track
- Put the right people in the right role
- Balance short-, mid- and long-term goals.

Appendix A Problem management policy template

This template provides the basic content for a problem management process policy. Specific policy statements, wording, content and structure will vary by organization, and the template should be modified accordingly.

Instructions

1. Review and complete all relevant sections in this template.
2. Remove all sections that are not relevant.
3. Add any missing sections.
4. Find and replace all <Company name> entries with your company name.
5. Find and replace or remove all other text in < > from the final draft of this document.
6. Adjust any verbiage as required to reflect unique requirements.
7. Add, if desired, a cover page.

Note that this document is for reference use only and should be viewed as an example, not a final document to meet the needs of all IT organizations. Final content is the sole responsibility of the author.

Problem management policy

Introduction and scope

This policy pertains to the <Company name> IT problem management process. For the purpose of this policy, a 'problem' is the cause or potential cause of incidents where the root cause is not usually known.

Purpose

The purpose of this policy is to formalize management direction and support for problem management best practices. Clear, consistent and realistic policies outline management expectations for employee responsibilities and actions.

Audience

The policy applies to all <Company name> IT personnel, whether permanent, temporary, or contractor, and anyone, including third-party vendors or suppliers, who has a stake in resolving any problems within the <Company name> IT computing environments. All personnel involved in resolving problems are responsible for compliance with the statements and directives set forth in this document.

Policy objectives

This policy is intended to achieve the following objectives:

1. Provide guiding principles for the deployment of a problem management process within the <Company name> IT organization.
2. Establish accountability for execution and compliance of the process across IT.
3. Communicate the intent to use standardized performance measurements for the problem management process.
4. Communicate <Company name> IT management's vision and expectation of achieving, over a period of time, reduced business impact of problems by timely resolution and prevention, thereby increasing IT service delivery effectiveness and service availability.

<Company name> IT has established an active programme for achieving problem management objectives in order to improve the availability and reliability of IT services.

Key components and objectives of this programme are to:

1. Establish a formal problem management process within <Company name> IT with clearly defined roles and responsibilities for creating, implementing and maintaining a best-practice-based problem management set of activities and practices.
2. Formally document the problem management process through the creation of a process policy, plan and standard operating procedure (SOP).
3. Ensure that appropriate support personnel are trained on problem management activities and tool(s).
4. Use an integrated tool that supports inter-process relationships and requirements between problem management and incident, change and configuration management.
5. Ensure that accurate problem management reporting is accomplished and that analysis of these reports drives continual improvement.

Appendix A: Problem management policy template

Policy statements

Background

<Company name> IT exists to enable and assist <Company name> businesses in achieving their stated objectives. As business needs and client expectations increase, the availability and reliability of IT-provided services is essential. <Company name> IT is adapting industry best practices for problem management in order to better meet the objectives required by the business.

Primary statements

<Company name> IT senior management makes the following statements with regard to problem management:

1. Directors, managers, supervisors and team leads are responsible to ensure that relevant IT staff members are suitably trained to support this policy.

2. All problem management documentation – policy, plan and SOP – shall be maintained within the <Company name> IT <document management system> and shall be accessible to IT staff.

3. IT senior management shall assign a problem management process owner and process manager, key roles within problem management, who will be accountable for organizational development, quality, implementation and performance of the process, including policies, procedures and training.

4. Problem management shall provide a single definition of a problem that will be common and used throughout IT and other IT service management processes.

5. Only one problem management process based on industry best practices shall exist and be used throughout the organization, regardless of the location where problem management activities may be performed.

6. Only one tool suite shall be used for the logging and tracking of problems, regardless of how or where the problems are detected. A knowledge base or known error database will be used to store workarounds.

7. All identified or reported problems shall be formally logged within the <Company name> IT service management tool.

8. A problem record is opened when there is an incident for which the root cause is not known. However, a problem record must be opened when one of the following criteria exists:

Problem Management

    a. Multiple incidents showing the same symptoms where the cause is unknown

    b. Any incident that is assigned a priority 1 or where a major incident has been identified

    c. Validated alarms from monitoring devices that are deemed high impact

    d. Any incident that is opened as a result of a security incident. A security incident can include, but is not limited to, the following:

- Viruses
- Trojans
- Worms
- Malware
- Unauthorized access.

9. All problems will be prioritized and categorized using the same prioritization and categorization models that have been defined for incident management.

10. All problem records will be assigned to a work queue of an appropriate technical support group. The problem queue manager for that work queue will assign the problem record to a specific person who will be responsible for finding the root cause, a workaround and, ideally, a permanent fix. At no stage should a problem record be assigned to a work group for open-ended pick-up.

11. Technical support group members are expected to use structured root cause analysis techniques when investigating and diagnosing assigned problems.

12. Each technical support group member who is assigned to work on a problem will be responsible for updating the problem record according to the parameters defined within the problem management process plan or SOP.

13. Incident management will attempt to match incidents to known errors or problems. During the problem identification and logging activity, problem management will also attempt to match incidents to existing known errors or problems.

14. Problem management will review, approve and submit workarounds for publication that have been submitted by incident management or by technical support groups.

15. All major incident occurrences will require a problem resolution team to be formed to identify root cause and determine actions to be taken to prevent such future occurrences. The team will be led by the problem manager, team lead, or technical support group manager.

16. After successful identification of the root cause and a workaround or temporary fix, the problem record will be changed from a problem record to a known error.

Appendix A: Problem management policy template

17. Decisions to resolve or refrain from resolving a problem should be approved by both the business and IT. Decisions should be documented in the problem record and communicated to appropriate stakeholders.
18. A request for change (RFC) must be submitted to change management for the approval to remove the error from the infrastructure. Change, release and problem management shall work together to ensure the implementation and verification of the permanent solution.
19. Known errors and problem records will only be closed after verification that incidents related to the problem or known error are no longer occurring.
20. Problem management reports will be provided to designated stakeholders in accordance with defined procedures outlined in the process plan or SOP and any formal service level agreements.
21. Problem reviews will be conducted on a frequency determined by the process owner and process manager. Reviews will focus on process compliance, quality, repeatability and key performance indicators (KPIs). Recommendations from these reviews should be published and distributed to IT management.

Roles and responsibilities

Problem management roles and responsibilities are defined in detail within the problem management process plan document. Problem management process activities are detailed within the problem management SOP document. These documents are located in the <document management system>.

Policy compliance

All IT personnel are expected to be actively involved in maintaining problem management best practices in accordance with this policy. Conduct deemed in violation of this policy may result in disciplinary corrective action. Any employee aware of violations of this policy is responsible for reporting such violations to the appropriate manager.

Policy approval and tracking information	
Approval(s): <Name>, <Title>	Date: <Date>
Author(s): <Name>, <Title>	
Next review date: <Date>	Replaces policy(ies) named and dated: <Name>, <Date>

Appendix B Sample problem management plan table of contents

Introduction

Goal

Purpose

Key definitions

High-level process documentation

Problem management high-level process flow diagram

Problem management process relationships diagram

Problem management major process activities

Detection and classification

    Identification and recording

    Categorization and resource allocation

Investigation and diagnosis

    Investigate and diagnose

Resolution and recovery

    Solution identification

    Solution implementation

Closure

    Problem and error closure

Problem management roles and responsibilities

Process measures and management reporting

Common problem management key performance indicators

<Company name> measures and management reports

Training and tools

Training

Problem management tools and access profiles

Appendix C Problem management standard operating procedures template

This template provides the content for a problem management process flow and standard operating procedures (SOPs) document. It is a basic problem management workflow and is not meant to be used 'as-is'. Specific SOP content and structure will vary by organization and the template should be modified accordingly. Each major activity in the workflow consists of numbered tasks that are tied to the work instructions within the SOP. In this workflow, the problem manager and problem queue manager are different roles.

Instructions

1. Review and complete all relevant sections in this template.
2. Remove all sections that are not relevant.
3. Add any missing sections.
4. Find and replace all <Company name> entries with your company name.
5. Find and replace or remove all other text in < > from the final draft of this document.
6. Adjust any template verbiage as required to reflect unique requirements.

Note that this document is for reference use only and should be viewed as an example, not a final document to meet the needs of all IT organizations. Final content is the sole responsibility of the author.

Problem Management

Standard operating procedures

<Paste company logo here> <Date>

Table of contents

Figure C.1 Problem management high-level process flow

Figure C.2 Problem management process relationships

Process activities introduction

Detection and categorization

Identification and recording

    How to search for a problem or known error record

    How to update the problem or known error record

    How to link an incident record to a problem or known error record

    How to open a problem record

Categorization and resource allocation

    How to complete a newly opened problem record

    How to link a duplicate problem record to the original problem record

    How to assign a problem record to another person

Investigation and diagnosis

Investigate and diagnose: Part 1

    How to update the problem record with the incident record resolution

Investigate and diagnose: Part 2

    How to edit the problem record and record the root cause

    How to link the problem or known error record to the CI at fault

Resolution and recovery

Solution identification

Solution implementation

    How to record the solution in the problem record

Closure

Problem and error closure

Addendum A: Criteria for a problem

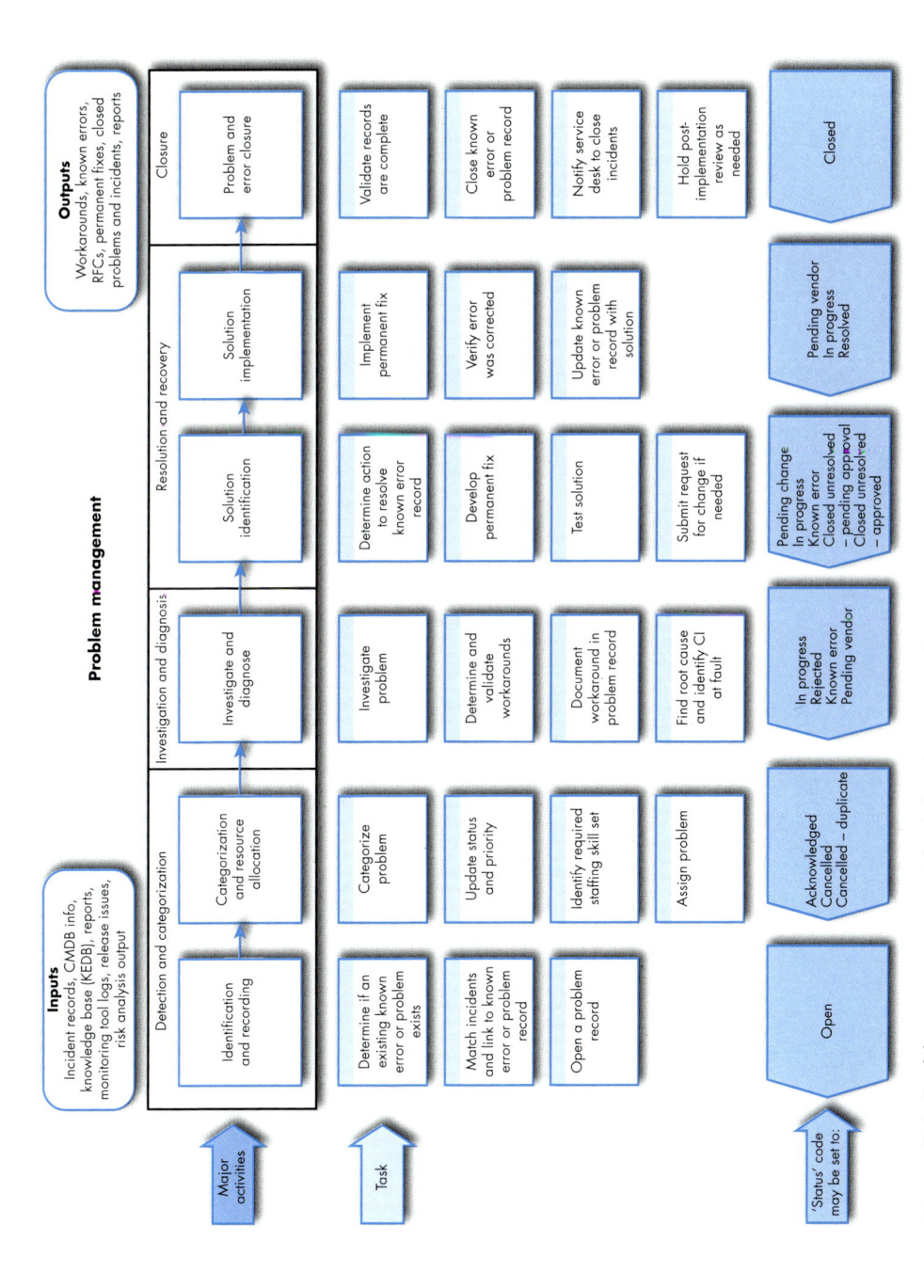

Figure C.1 Problem management high-level process flow

Problem Management

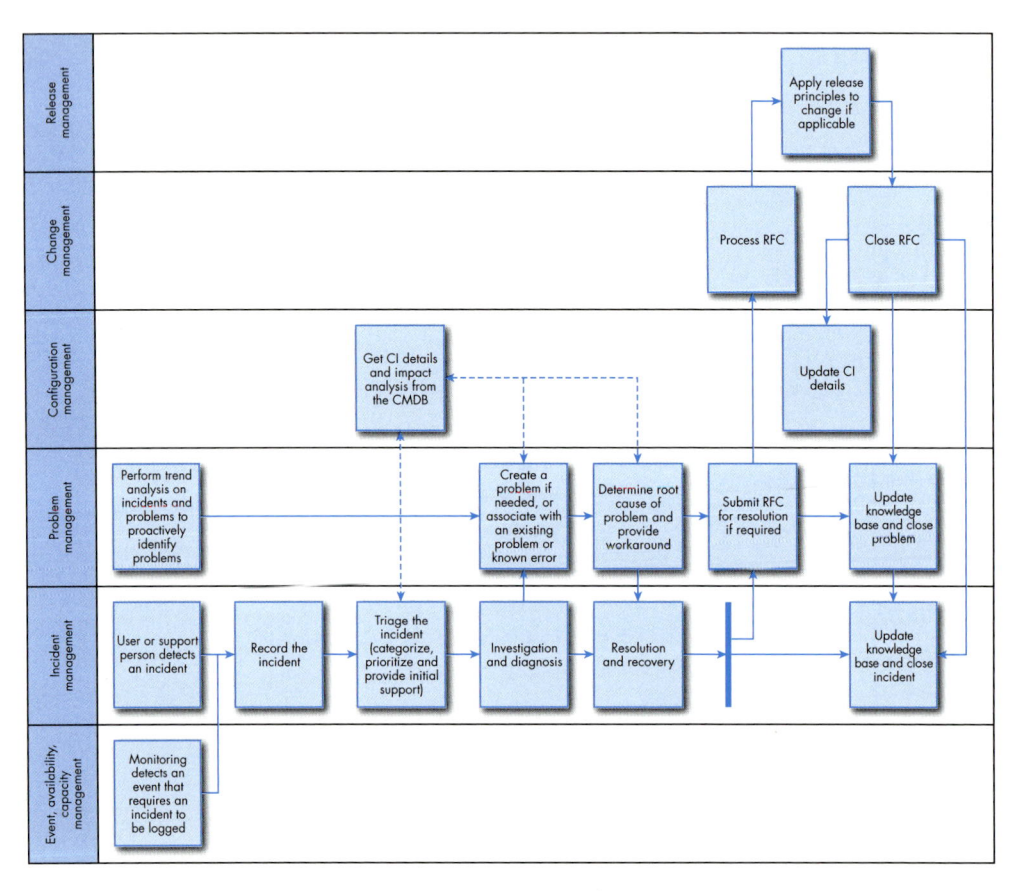

Figure C.2 Problem management process relationships

Process activities introduction

There are four major categories of activities within problem management:

- **Detection and categorization** Problem detection and categorization are those activities focused on identifying, logging and classifying problems.

    Activities recognized in detection and categorization are:

    - Problem identification and recording
    - Problem categorization and resource allocation.

- **Investigation and diagnosis** Problem investigation and diagnosis are those activities focused on identifying root cause and transforming problems into known errors. The goal is to identify the root cause and the configuration items (CIs) that are at fault, and to provide the service desk with information and advice on workarounds, when available.

- **Resolution and recovery** Problem resolution and recovery are those activities focused on identifying, approving, applying and validating permanent fixes to problems and known errors. These activities eliminate known errors by the successful implementation of a change under the control of the change management process. The objective is to have awareness of existing errors, monitor them and eliminate them when feasible and cost-justifiable.

    Activities recognized in resolution and recovery are:

    - Solution identification
    - Solution implementation.

- **Closure** Problem closure includes those activities focused on closing problems, known errors and related incidents with updated and reusable information. Following successful implementation of changes to resolve errors, the relevant known error or problem record is closed, together with any associated incident records. Verification of the problem resolution is necessary to ensure that the fixes have actually worked. A post-implementation review (PIR) confirms the effectiveness of the solution and captures lessons learned.

These four categories of activities are dealt with below and each category section includes a workflow diagram (see Figure C.3 for the symbols and abbreviations used) and notes on the individual tasks within the workflow.

There is one other major activity that is not part of the normal and daily flow for handling problems. This activity is called a 'major problem review'.

Major problem reviews are very detailed and focused on any problem where the impact to the organization was significant enough that management decides to review activities associated with the investigation, diagnosis and resolution of the problem. In essence, the actions and interactions of people, process and technology are reviewed and assessed.

Both normal and major problem reviews are conducted as part of the closure activity.

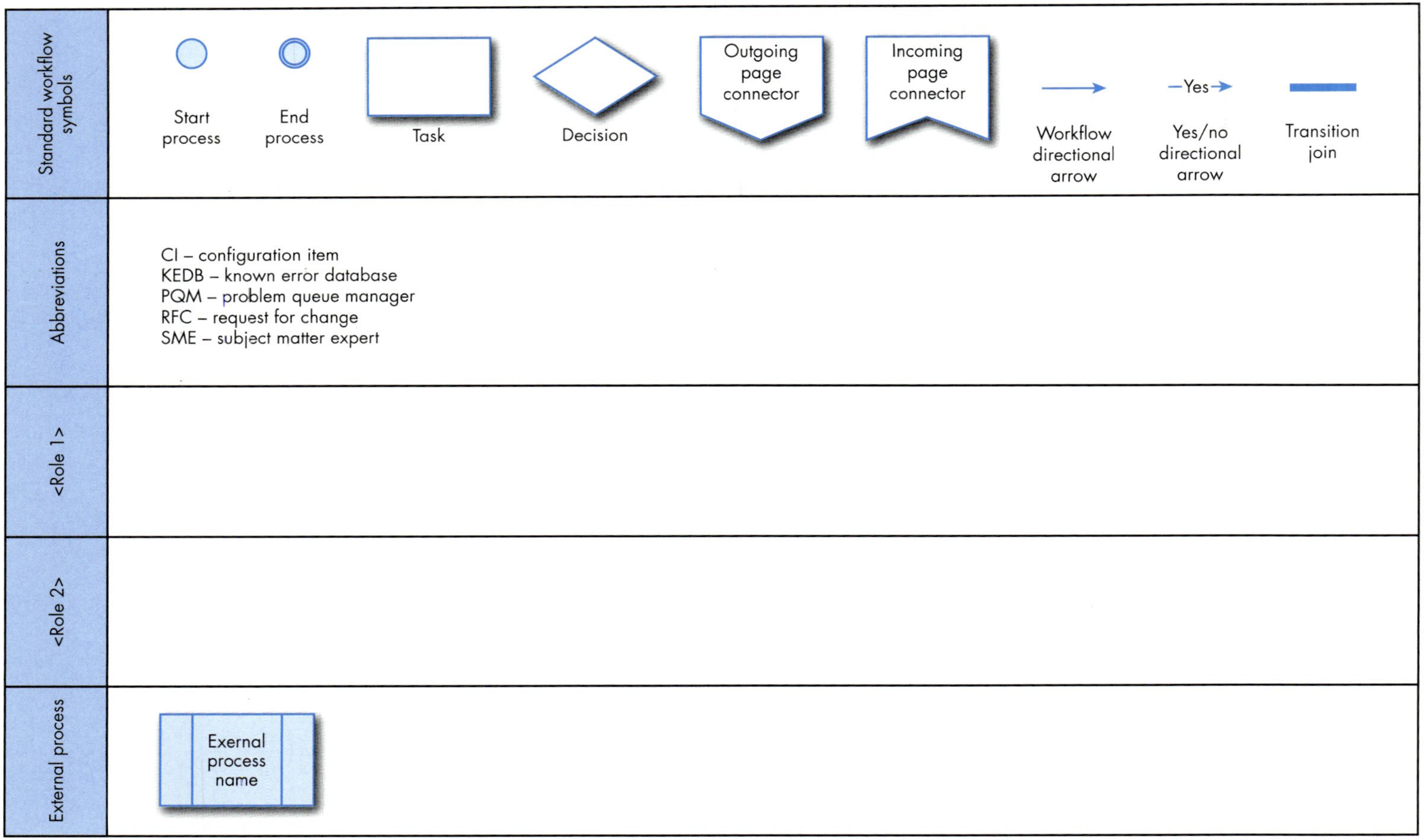

Standard workflow symbols	Start process ○ End process ◎ Task □ Decision ◇ Outgoing page connector Incoming page connector ↑ Workflow directional arrow —Yes→ Yes/no directional arrow ▮ Transition join
Abbreviations	CI – configuration item KEDB – known error database PQM – problem queue manager RFC – request for change SME – subject matter expert
<Role 1>	
<Role 2>	
External process	External process name

Figure C.3 Standard workflow symbols and abbreviations used within the workflow

Detection and categorization

Identification and recording (see Figure C.4)

PRB.02.05 A technical support group subject matter expert (SME) identifies a potential problem during trending of incidents or through observation of the live environment.

PRB.02.10 Incidents may be detected by users or IT staff, or event, availability and capacity management monitoring tools or personnel. The service desk will be contacted or the web portal used to open an incident record and the record will be assigned to a support group.

PRB.02.15 A support group SME assesses the situation and determines if the information available indicates a potential problem. If an incident record was assigned, the SME resolves the incident first and then determines if a potential problem exists. If a problem does not exist, this is the end of the process.

PRB.02.20 The support group SME has determined that a potential problem exists. The SME then searches for a problem or known error record to determine if one already exists. If one is found, the SME updates the record with any new information or links the new incident record to the existing problem or known error record using one of the procedures described below.

How to search for a problem or known error record

1. <Click on …>
2. <The following screen will appear>

   <Insert screenshot here>

<Continue on with instructions and add screenshots …>

If a problem or known error record is found and you have a new incident related to this problem, follow the steps below in 'How to link an incident record to a problem or known error record'. Otherwise, if you have any updates (additional occurrences or symptoms) that would be helpful to annotate on the problem record, follow the steps below to update the problem or known error record.

How to update the problem or known error record

1. <Click on …>
2. <The following screen will appear>

   <Insert screenshot here>

<Continue on with instructions and add screenshots …>

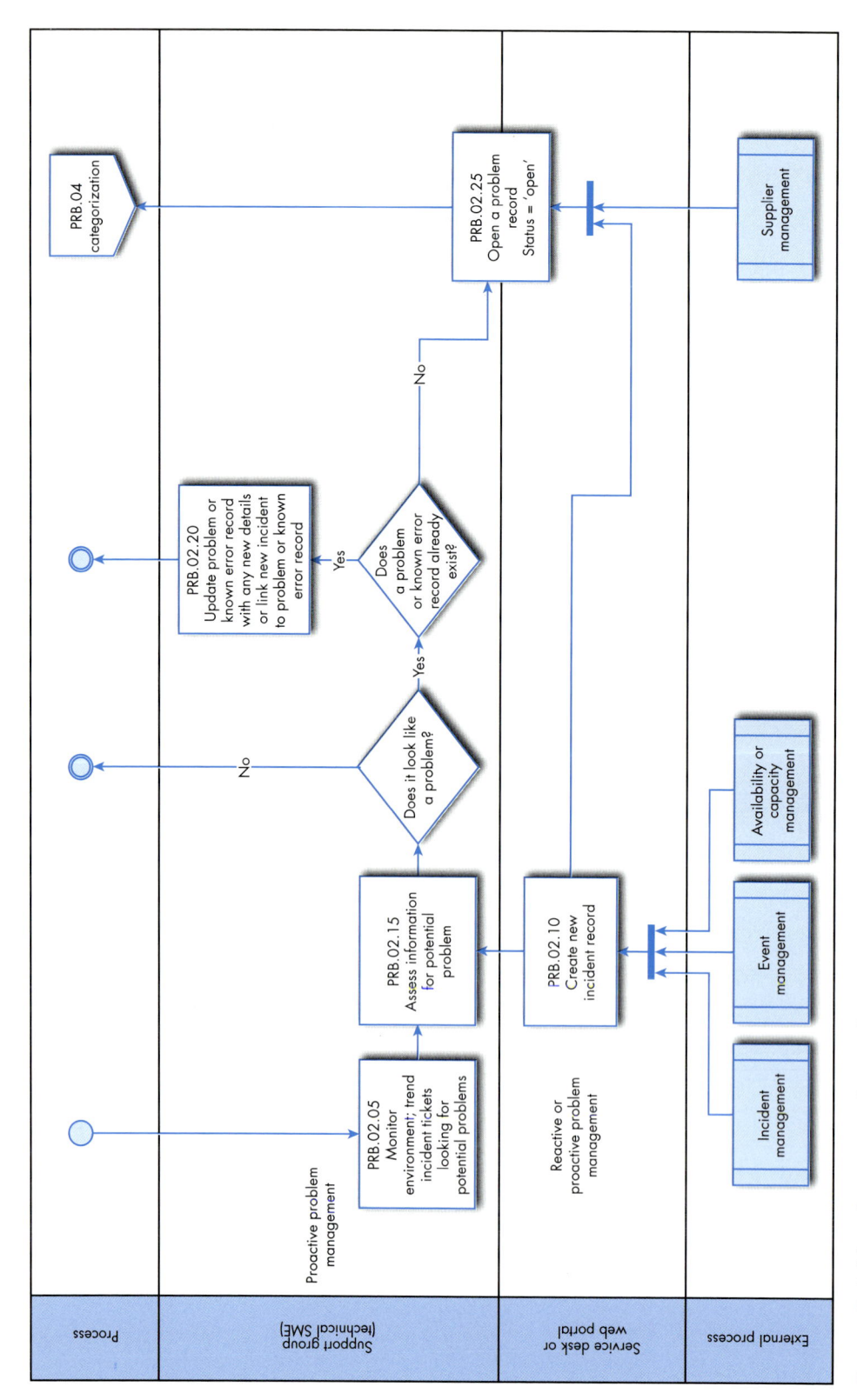

Figure C.4 Identification and recording

Appendix C: Problem management standard operating procedures template

How to link an incident record to a problem or known error record
1. <Click on ...>
2. <The following screen will appear>

    <Insert screenshot here>

<Continue on with instructions and add screenshots ...>

PRB.02.25 If a problem record needs to be created, then follow the steps below to open a problem record.

How to open a problem record
1. <Click on ...>
2. <The following screen will appear>

    <Insert screenshot here>

<Continue on with instructions and add screenshots ...>

Categorization and resource allocation (see Figure C.5)

PRB.04.05 After opening a problem record, fill in the required fields on the new problem record by following the steps described below.

How to complete a newly opened problem record
1. <Click on ...>
2. <The following screen will appear>

    <Insert screenshot here>

<Continue on with instructions and add screenshots ...>

PRB.04.10, **PRB.04.15**, **PRB.04.20**, **PRB.04.25** and **PRB.04.30** The problem queue manager (PQM) should regularly check for problem records in the work queue that have not been assigned. When such a record is found, the PQM should change the status to 'acknowledged' and save the record. The PQM will assess whether the record is a duplicate or if the record is truly a problem that needs to be worked on. If the conclusion is that the record is not a true problem (see Addendum A), change the status to 'cancelled' and notify the problem record creator and the service desk. If the record is a duplicate problem record, the PQM should change the status to 'cancelled – duplicate', link the duplicate problem record to the original problem record, and notify the problem record creator and service desk. Perform the steps as described below for linking the duplicate problem record to the original problem record.

Problem Management

How to link a duplicate problem record to the original problem record
1. <Click on ...>
2. <The following screen will appear>

    <Insert screenshot here>

<Continue on with instructions and add screenshots ...>

PRB.04.35, PRB.04.40, PRB.04.45 and **PRB.04.50** If the problem is not a duplicate, the PQM should assess the problem record and, based on the information available, identify the skill set and team member capable of performing the investigation and diagnosis. The PQM then assigns the record to a team member by performing the steps as described below.

How to assign a problem record to another person
1. <Click on ...>
2. <The following screen will appear>

    <Insert screenshot here>

<Continue on with instructions and add screenshots...>

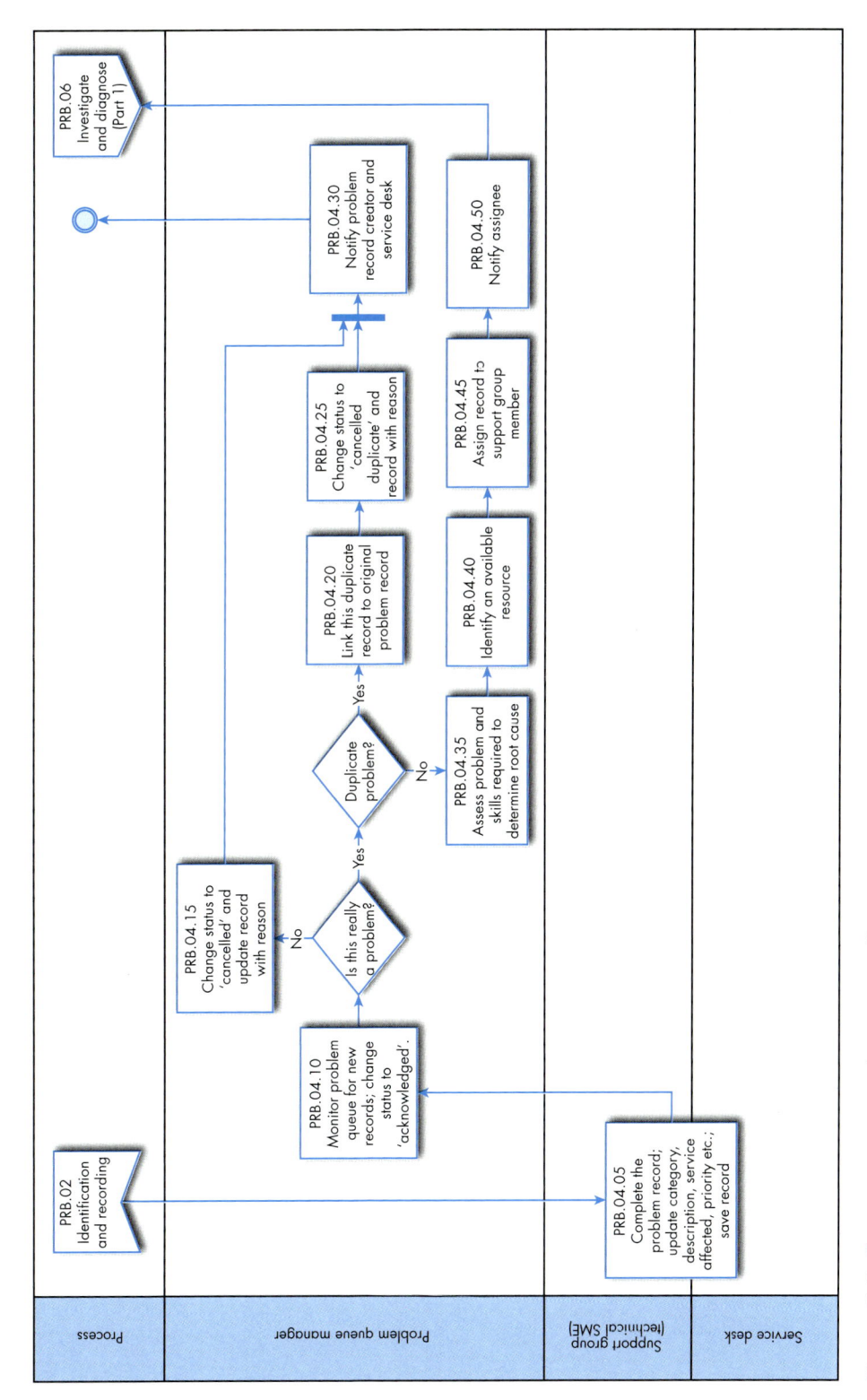

Figure C.5 Categorization and resource allocation

Investigation and diagnosis

Investigate and diagnose: Part 1 (see Figure C.6)

PRB.06.05 When the assigned support group SME receives the problem record, he/she changes the status to 'in progress'.

PRB.06.10 If the SME believes the incident record resolution would make a valid workaround, they update the problem record with the workaround from the incident record.

How to update the problem record with the incident record resolution
1. <Click on ...>
2. <The following screen will appear>

    <Insert screenshot here>

<Continue on with instructions and add screenshots...>

PRB.06.15 If the SME believes the incident record resolution would not make a valid workaround, the SME searches for a valid workaround and, if one is found, they update the problem record with the workaround by following the steps listed above for PRB.06.10.

PRB.06.20 The SME assigns the record to the PQM for validation and approval of the workaround. Assign the record to the PQM using the procedure identified in PRB.04.45, above.

PRB.06.25, PRB.06.30, PRB.06.35 The PQM reviews and discusses the proposed workaround with the SME. If the PQM deems the workaround a valid workaround, the PQM will publish the workaround to the knowledge base or known error database (KEDB) and assign the record back to the SME to perform root cause analysis. If the workaround is not deemed valid, the PQM will assign the record back to the SME for further research and identification of a workaround.

PRB.06.40 If the SME cannot determine a valid workaround, the SME documents this in the problem record.

PRB.06.45 The SME begins investigating and diagnosing the problem, looking for the root cause, using root cause analysis techniques, researching websites and (as necessary) working with the vendor. This may require an individual effort or may require pulling together a team of SMEs to assist in the investigation and diagnosis of the problem.

PRB.06.50 If, during the investigating and diagnosing of the problem, the SME cannot determine the root cause **and** determines that the problem record is misassigned, **or** if the 'investigation, diagnosis and resolution team' determines that the problem record is misassigned, update the problem record with the reason and assign the record to the problem manager for reassignment.

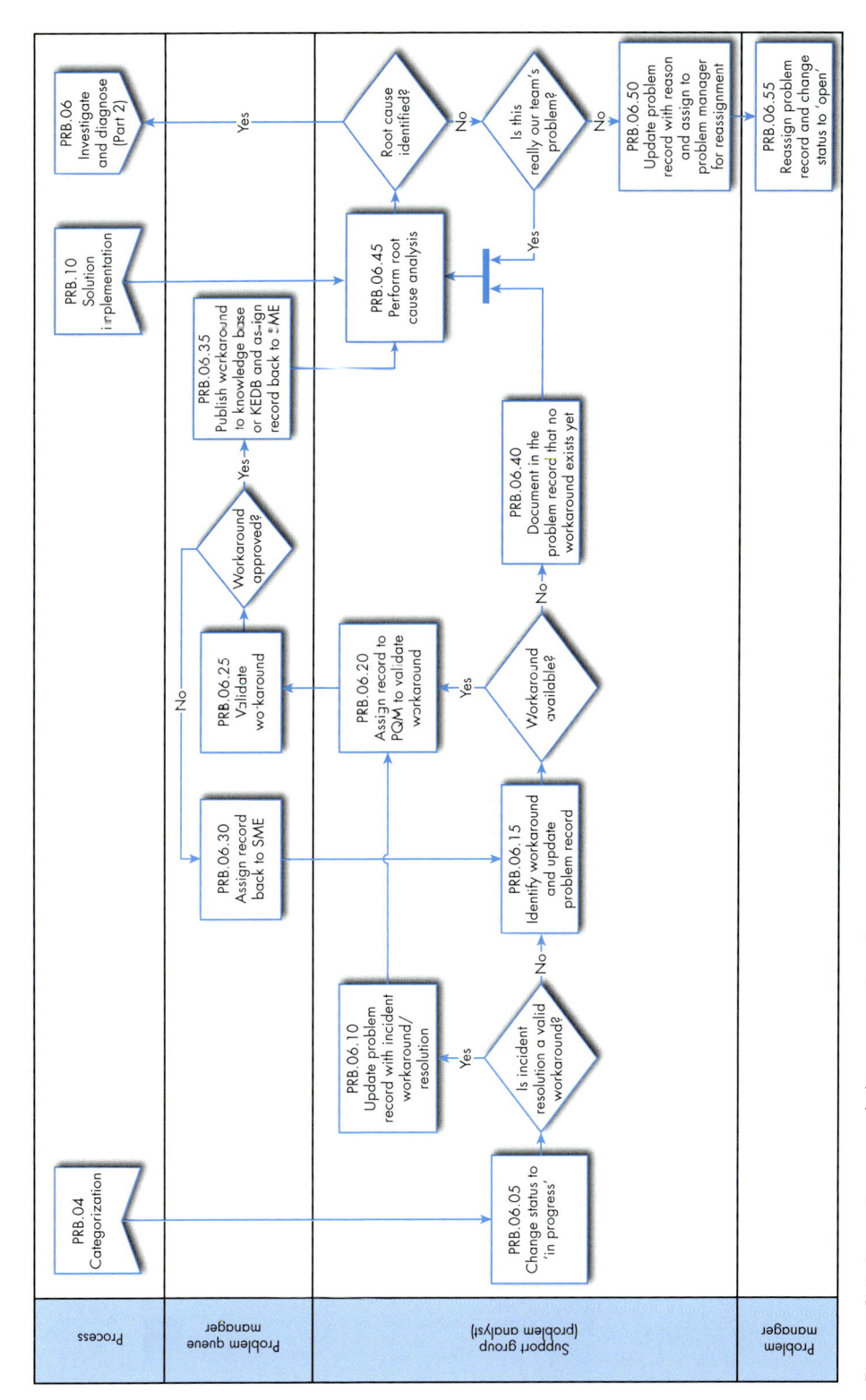

Figure C.6 Investigate and diagnose: Part 1

PRB.06.55 The problem manager should review the problem record for comments regarding the request for reassignment and then reassign the problem record to the appropriate group. If the problem manager does not think the problem record should be reassigned to a different group, the problem manager should discuss this with the PQM and then reassign the ticket back to the SME.

Investigate and diagnose: Part 2 (see Figure C.7)

PRB.06.60 When a root cause is discovered, assign a root cause to the problem record.

PRB.06.65 and PRB.06.70 If this is a request for new functionality (i.e. someone identified a 'problem' because they thought the system should be doing something it was not designed to do), change the status to 'problem rejected', update the problem record with your reason and save the record. Notify the PQM and the service desk of your action.

How to edit the problem record and record the root cause
1. <Click on …>
2. <The following screen will appear>

    <Insert screenshot here>

<Continue on with instructions and add screenshots …>

PRB.06.75 If this is not a request for new functionality and a workaround is available, change the status to 'known error' (now that the root cause **and** a workaround has been identified).

PRB.06.80 and PRB.06.85 When a root cause is discovered, the SME should link the problem or known error record to the CI at fault by performing the following steps.

How to link the problem or known error record to the CI at fault
1. <Click on …>
2. <The following screen will appear>

    <Insert screenshot here>

<Continue on with instructions and add screenshots …>

PRB.06.90, PRB.06.95 If only a vendor can fix this problem, report the problem to the vendor and change the status of the record to 'pending vendor'. Notify the PQM and the service desk of your action.

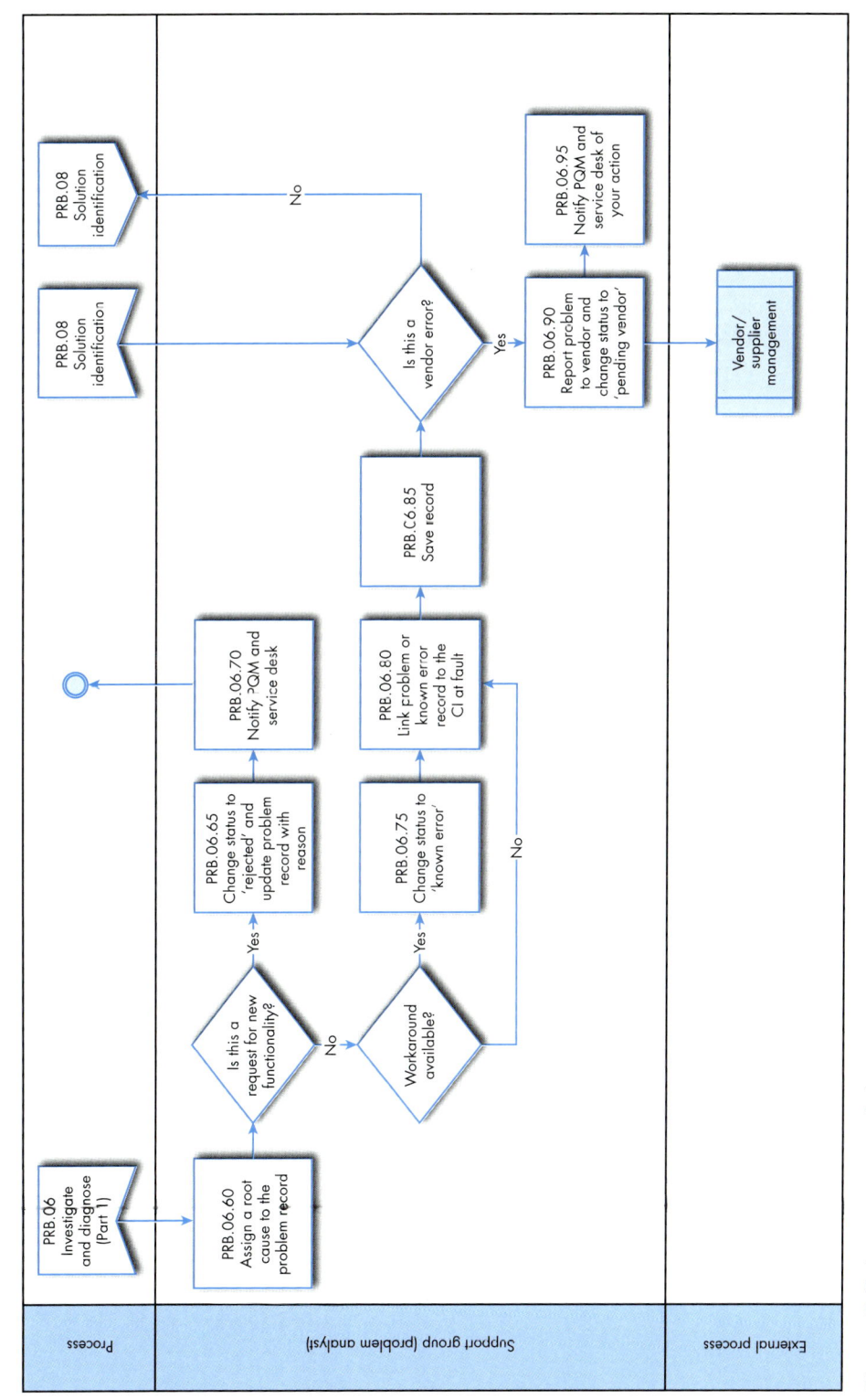

Figure C.7 Investigate and diagnose: Part 2

Resolution and recovery

Solution identification (see Figure C.8)

PRB.08.05 Identify, evaluate and conclude what actions are required to permanently resolve this problem or known error. This may require an individual effort or may require pulling together a team of SMEs to assess and determine a permanent fix.

PRB.08.10 If the permanent fix requires that a request for change (RFC) be submitted, follow the process for submitting the RFC and change the status of the record to 'pending change'. The permanent fix will follow the change and release management processes which include the development and testing of the permanent fix.

PRB.08.15 and PRB.08.20 If the SME determines that the problem cannot be repeated or resolved, change the status of the record to 'closed unresolved – pending approval'. Document the reason and efforts expended in trying to resolve the problem in the problem record, and assign the record to the problem manager for approval.

PRB.08.25 If the problem manager determines that the problem needs further research, or that a permanent fix should be determined and implemented, he/she discusses this decision with the PQM, changes the status back to 'in progress' or 'known error' (depending on whether there is a workaround or not), and assigns the record back to the SME for further research and work.

PRB.08.30 If the problem manager determines that a solution to the problem has been sufficiently researched but no resolution is available, he/she will change the status to 'closed unresolved – approved'.

PRB.08.35 The service desk will monitor its queue for all 'closed unresolved – approved' records and will then close all related incidents for those records and make any necessary communications to users.

PRB.08.40 and PRB.08.45 There may be situations where a fix can be applied without having to go through change management (e.g. improving communications or training, or based on organizational decisions). In such cases where an RFC is not needed (which should be rare), proceed to develop the permanent fix. Test the permanent fix before applying it to the production environment. If the test shows that the fix would be successful in resolving the problem, proceed to implementing the fix. Otherwise return to PRB.06 Investigate and diagnose.

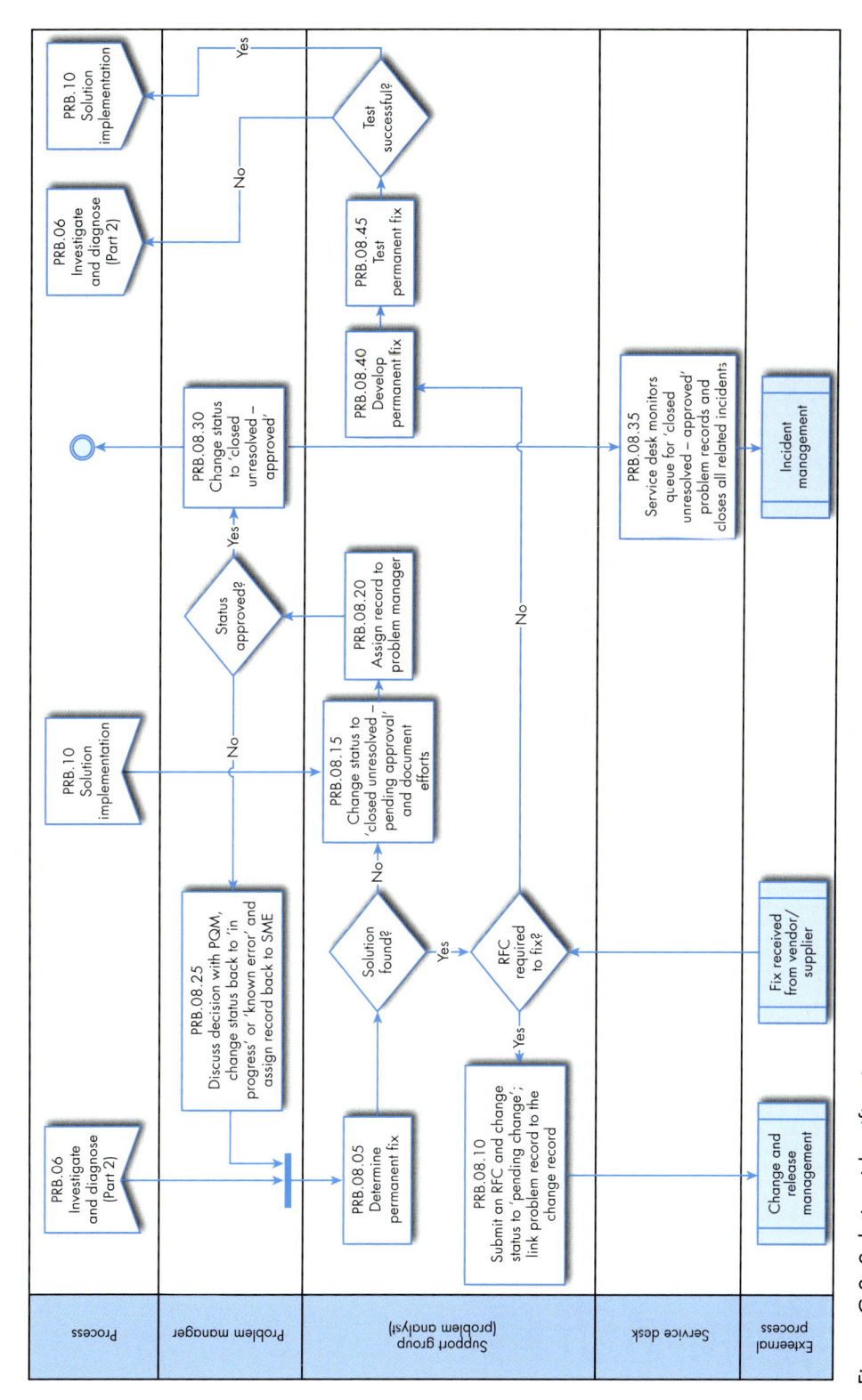

Figure C.8 Solution identification

Solution implementation (see Figure C.9)

PRB.10.05 If implementation approval of the permanent solution was denied, or if the permanent solution was rejected by the business, document the decision in the problem record and proceed to seek approval for marking the record as closed and unresolved.

PRB.10.10 If implementation approval has been given, implement the change into production. This will typically be done through the use of the release and deployment management process. Validate that the error was removed by the permanent fix.

PRB.10.15 If the error was resolved, change the status of the record to 'resolved' and record the solution in the problem record, using the following steps.

How to record the solution in the problem record
1. <Click on …>
2. <The following screen will appear>

   <Insert screenshot here>

<Continue on with instructions and add screenshots …>

PRB.10.20 If the error was not resolved and the fix did not come from a vendor, change the status of the record to 'in progress' and return to PRB.06 investigate and diagnose. If the error was not resolved and it was a vendor-supplied fix, escalate to the vendor.

PRB.10.25 and PRB.10.30 If the error was not resolved and the fix came from a vendor, change the status of the record to 'pending vendor' and contact the vendor to request a new fix. Notify the PQM and the service desk of your action.

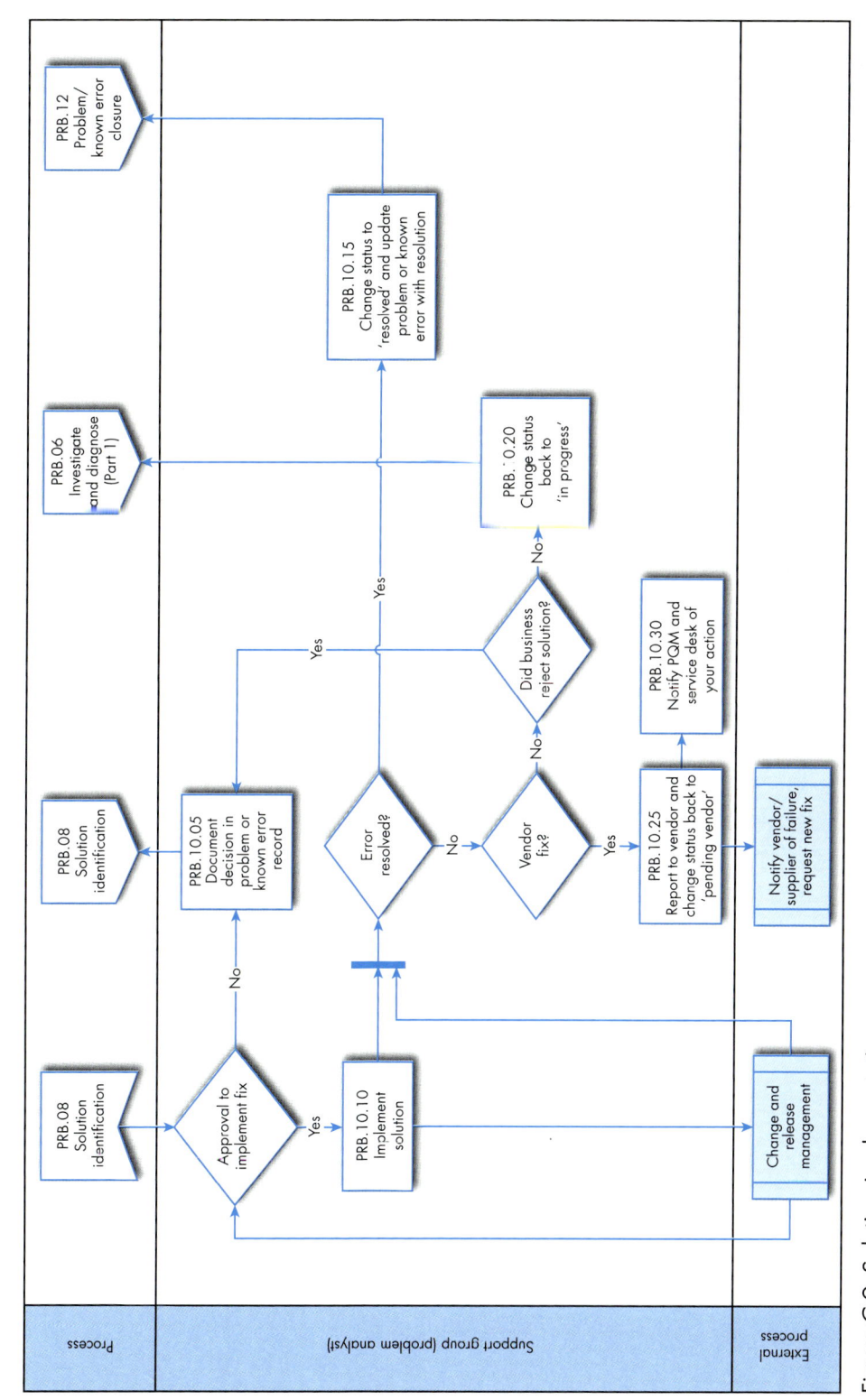

Figure C.9 Solution implementation

Closure

Problem and known error closure (see Figure C.10)

PRB.12.05 The support group SME should review the problem record, ensuring that all fields are updated with current and correct information. The SME also ensures the right CIs are linked to the problem record.

PRB.12.10 Assign the problem record to the PQM for a quality review.

PRB.12.15, PRB.12.20 and PRB.12.25 The PQM will review the problem record for completeness and accuracy. If the record is of good quality, the PQM will change the status to 'closed'. Otherwise, assign the record back to the SME with comments to improve the completeness and accuracy of the record.

PRB.12.30 The service desk closes all related incidents.

PRB.12.35 Based on the organizational criteria for when to perform a post-implementation review of a problem, the problem manager, PQM, support group SMEs and the service desk participate in a review of the problem for capturing lessons learned and for determining where improvements in people, process and technology can be implemented.

Addendum A: Criteria for a problem

A problem record is opened when there is an incident or potential incident for which the root cause is not known. However, a problem record must be opened when one of the following criteria exists:

<Add criteria here ...>

A support group may choose to cancel a problem record assigned to them which does not meet the above criteria or which fits the criteria below. This decision should only be made by the PQM. The additional criteria for assessing whether a problem record truly reflects a problem are:

- The record appears to be frivolous or created in error (e.g. an incident record was created for a high impact 'false-positive' alarm which in turn required a problem record be created)
- It appears that events were misinterpreted by an SME or service desk agent, or a wrong conclusion was drawn of the events.

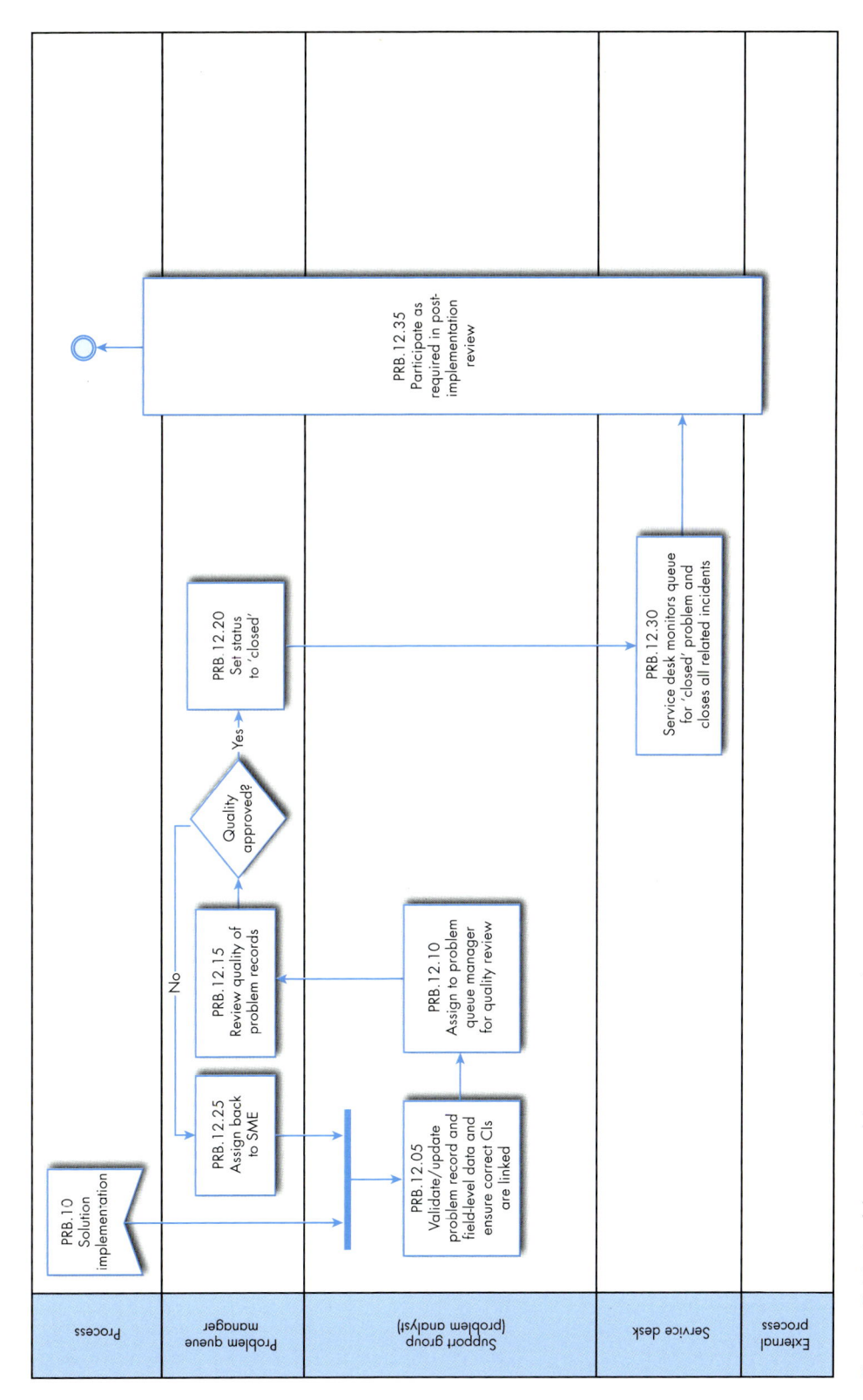

Figure C.10 Problem and known error closure

Appendix D Examples of symptom, resolution and root cause codes

The following tables provide examples of a set of symptom, resolution and root cause codes for incidents and problems.

Note that these tables are for reference use only and should be viewed as an example, not a template to meet the needs of all IT organizations. Specific content and structure will vary by organization.

Table D.1 Sample symptom codes for incidents and problems

Symptom code	Indications
Access denied	The identified object cannot be accessed or logged into
Alert	An alert, alarm or error message has occurred
Cannot access	There is a connectivity issue with the identified object
Cannot print	The user is not able to print within the application
Capacity	The identified object has exceeded a threshold or is out of capacity
Data	There are issues on the completeness, accuracy or validity of the data
Down	The identified object is down, out or locked-up
Image	The identified object has no image or a poor image
Intermittent	The identified object is failing intermittently
Missing	The identified object is missing or lost
Monitoring alert	A monitoring exception or alert has occurred
Not faxing	A fax machine is not working
Not printing	A printer is not printing
Not scanning	A user is having trouble scanning within the application or using a scanner
Paper jamming	A printer is jamming
Poor print quality	The printer ink quality is bad, streaking etc.
Slow response	There are slow response times to the identified object
Virus	The identified object may have a virus, Trojan, malware etc.

Table D.2 Sample resolution codes for incidents and problems

Resolution code	Meaning
Access granted	Access was granted to the identified object
Alert resolved	The identified monitoring exception or alert has been resolved
Backed-up/recovered	The identified object has been recovered or backed-up
Capacity corrected	The capacity threshold for the identified object has been restored to normal levels
Configured	Configuration changes were made to the identified object
Connectivity restored	Connectivity issue with the identified object has been resolved
Installed	Installation of the identified object has been completed
Maintained	Maintenance to the identified object has been completed
Moved	Relocation of the identified object has been completed
Rebooted	The identified object has been rebooted or restarted to resolve issues
Removed	Removal of the identified object has been completed
Removed paper jam	Paper jam was corrected
Replaced	Replacement of the identified object has been completed
Replaced toner	Toner cartridge was replaced
Restored	Availability has been restored to the identified object
Updated/patched	Updates/patches have been applied to the identified object
Virus removed	The virus, Trojan, malware etc. was removed from the identified object

Appendix D: Examples of symptom, resolution and root cause codes

Table D.3 Sample root cause codes for incidents and problems

Root cause code	Meaning
Access	Access was never granted; access had been removed; password expired; drive not mapped
Bug	A failure in the code of an application or software component (e.g. scripting error, software defect, microcode defect etc.)
Capacity	Over-used CI resulting in degraded performance or failure
Configuration	A hardware, software, firmware or network configuration problem that has caused an interruption of a system or service; an architectural design flaw
Data corruption	A database or file had a data integrity issue
Documentation	Documentation was missing or out of date (e.g. process, procedural, technical, on-call list etc.)
Environmental	Temperature, moisture or other environmental causes
Hardware	A failure of a physical CI (e.g. server failed, router failed, batteries died, hard drive failed)
Internet	A failure caused by a conflicting IP or ISP outage
IT action	An action taken by IT that caused an interruption of a system or service
Malware	Malicious code (e.g. virus, worm, Trojan etc.) within the computing environment
No problem	This was not a valid problem; this is a duplicate record; the CI is working as designed; the requested function/feature is not available
Other	The root cause is not listed in the drop-down list
Network	A failure related to an internal or external network segment
Power	Lack of, or interruption to, electrical power
Software	An outdated or incompatible version of software was in use; missing a software patch
Training	A lack of training on how to use the technology or process involved
Unknown	Root cause cannot be found or the problem cannot be reproduced
User action	An action taken by a non-IT user or customer that caused an interruption of a system or service (e.g. unplugged cable, moved equipment etc.)
Third-party action	A change made by a third party that caused an interruption of a system or service

Appendix E Two-tier categorization scheme example

Table E.1 provides an example of a two-tier incident and problem categorization scheme. Note that this table is for reference use only and should be viewed as an example, not a template to meet the needs of all IT organizations. Specific content and structure will vary by organization.

Table E.1 Sample two-tier incident and problem categorization scheme

Category	Subcategory
Facilities	Air conditioning
	Fire control
	Other
	Power
	UPS
Hardware	Audiovisual
	Desktop
	Laptop
	Logical partition
	Mainframe
	Mobile device
	Monitor
	Other
	Printer/scanner/copier/fax
	Server
	Storage
	Virtual machine
Network	Firewall
	Load balancer
	Other
	Router
	Switch
	Wireless
Security	Application
	Building
	Data
	Other

Table continues

Table E.1 *continued*

Category	Subcategory
Software	Application
	Database
	Internet
	Operating system
	Other
Telecom	Desktop phone
	Other
	Voice

Appendix F Service disruption report example

The following report provides an example of the basic content of a service disruption report.

Note that this report is for reference use only and should be viewed as an example, not a template to meet the needs of all IT organizations. Specific content and structure will vary by organization.

Company XYZ – Service disruption report

Service interruption – Mortgage loan administration

Start date/time and resolution date/time of outage

Start date and time	Resolution date and time
07.45 a.m. GMT, 12 April 2016	10.55 a.m. GMT, 12 April 2016

Customers affected

Mortgage Application System (MAS) customers

Outage summary

For approximately 3 hours and 10 minutes, the MAS primary database server went offline causing the MAS application software to hang up and preventing new users from logging on. At its peak, this affected approximately 400 users of the MAS application. The root cause was improperly configured antivirus software that was installed on the database server.

Outage details

- **05.00** Antivirus application software was installed on all MAS servers.
- **07.45** Several MAS clients called the service desk reporting an inability to log on. Error message stated 'Unable to process request'.
- **07.55** The server support team was assigned the ticket for resolution.
- **08.23** The antivirus software was identified as the cause.
- **08.26** Rollback of the antivirus software began.
- **08.44** Rollback of the antivirus software completed successfully.
- **08.48** Restart of the server began.
- **09.08** The server became available.

- **09.10** Recovery of the database began.
- **10.48** The MAS database was restored successfully.
- **10.50** The MAS application was started.
- **10.55** Mortgage loan administration service became available. Confirmation received that clients were able to log on.

Impact and severity of the outage

Clients received errors when attempting to logon to MAS. This resulted in approximately 400 users being unable to process loans and conduct business on the mortgage loan administration system.

Root cause

At 5.00 a.m. antivirus software was installed on all MAS production servers without first having been released to the testing environment. The antivirus software was not configured to exclude the database files, resulting in all service threads to the databases being consumed as users logged on, which in turn caused the databases to lock up when being accessed.

Method of restoration

The antivirus software was uninstalled from the database server.

Future prevention (to be completed by 15 April 2016)

After conducting an internal review of the outage, the following actions will be taken to prevent recurrence:

- Configure the antivirus software template to exclude all database folders on database servers.
- Install monitoring software to detect and alert when service thread use reaches 75% or greater.
- Implement process controls to ensure all changes are released through the testing environment.

Appendix G Sample project plan for process implementation

Table G.1 is a sample project plan that can be used when first designing and implementing a process. It can also be used as the basis for improving an existing process. Note that the start and end dates, projected duration and process roles (to the right across the top) are provided as typical examples, but will need to be adjusted and modified to the needs and culture of each IT organization. The numbers in the role columns represent an estimated number of hours to be spent on the task. Note also that some tasks have letters and numbers within square brackets. These denote templates that can be used in the delivery of that task. These templates are not included as part of this appendix.

Table G.1 Project plan for designing and implementing a process

BA = business analyst; CS = communication specialist; FTE = full-time equivalent; PM = process manager; PMP = project manager; PO = process owner; PT = process testers; TA = tool architect; WBS = work breakdown structure; WIP = work in progress

Task name	Duration	Start date (dd/mm)	Finish date (dd/mm)	PO	PM	PMP	BA	TA	CS	PT
ITSM process design and deployment WBS	204 days	01/01	11/10							
INITIATE	10 days	01/01	14/01							
Identify process owner, process manager and project team	5 days	01/01	07/01	3	6	3				
Create project WIP site [INI03]	5 days	01/01	07/01		2					
Perform process maturity assessment and discovery of existing process artefacts and templates [INI01]	5 days	01/0	07/01	2	6	2	4			
Identify process gaps to close and determine scope [INI17]	5 days	01/01	07/01	2	4	2	2			
Complete process definition document [INI05]	5 days	08/01	14/01	2	4	2	1			
Draft project charter [INI07]	5 days	08/01	14/01	1	4	2	1	1	1	
Complete project plan template [INI09]	5 days	08/01	14/01	2	6	8				
Schedule and hold project planning meeting – review project charter and project plan with project team [INI21]	5 days	08/01	14/01	2	4	6	2	2	2	
Obtain project charter approval	5 days	08/01	14/01	1		1				
Develop process communication and awareness plan [INI11]	5 days	08/01	14/01		4	2	2		2	

Identify design/workshop team members and project resource requirements [INI13]	5 days	08/01	14/01	1	2	1
Schedule project meetings	5 days	08/01	14/01		1	1
Create and send stakeholder solicitation letter to managers [INI23]	5 days	08/01	14/01	1	1	1
Start and populate project issues, risks and action logs [INI12, INI15, INI19]	5 days	08/01	14/01		2	1
DESIGN	73 days	15/01	25/04			
Design preparation	19 days	15/01	08/02			
Create slide deck for process design kick-off workshop (schedule, pain points) [DPR01]	5 days	15/01	21/01	1	4	2
Create slide deck for process overview, process principles/policies workshop [DPR03, DPR29]	5 days	15/01	21/01	1	12	2
Create and send workshop meeting invitations, schedule workshops [DPR15–27]	5 days	29/01	04/02	1	4	2
Create slide deck for roles and responsibilities workshop [DPR05, DPR31]	5 days	22/01	28/01	1	16	2
Create 'straw man' process workflow diagrams with touchpoints to other processes [DPR33]	10 days	22/01	04/02	4	40	8
Create slide deck for process workflows workshop [DPR07, DPR09]	5 days	04/02	08/02			
Review high-level process model with process owner, process manager and key stakeholders for validation and approval	10 days	22/01	04/02	2	6	

Table continues

Table G.1 continued

Task name	Duration	Start date (dd/mm)	Finish date (dd/mm)	PO	PM	PMP	Role BA	TA	CS	PT
Design workshops	58 days	05/02	25/04							
Hold process design kick-off workshop (schedule, pain points, roles and responsibilities, process development approach)	4 days	05/02	08/02	1	2		1	2		
Hold process overview, process principles/policies workshop	5 days	11/02	15/02	1	2		1	2		
Hold roles and responsibilities workshop	4 days	18/02	21/02	2	4		2	4		
Hold process workflow workshop	5 days	22/02	28/02	4	8		4	8		
Create slide deck for RACI workshop [DPR11, DWK01]	9 days	05/02	15/02	1	4		1			
Create slide deck for use cases, requirements, metrics workshop [DPR13]	3 days	15/02	19/02	1	8		2			
Hold RACI workshop	3 days	20/02	22/02	2	4		2	4		
Hold use cases, requirements, metrics workshop [DWK09]	5 days	25/02	01/03	2	4		2	4		
Update process artefacts (principles, policies, roles and responsibilities, workflows, RACI, KPIs, metrics)	22 days	08/02	11/03	2	16		4			
Create use case list and use cases [DWK03, DWK05]	5 days	11/03	15/03	1	16		16			

Create requirements traceability matrix (RTM) [DWK07]	5 days	15/03	21/03	2	12	12	2
Determine and document training requirements [DWK11]	5 days	15/03	21/03	1	4	4	4
Determine and document testing requirements [DWK13]	5 days	15/03	21/03	1	4	4	4
Determine infrastructure and tool modification requirements	10 days	15/03	28/03				4
Perform gap analysis against existing tools	5 days	15/03	21/03	1	4	4	4
Develop and document tool strategy	5 days	22/03	28/03	1	2	2	10
Submit hardware/software purchase requirements to IT procurement [DWK19]	5 days	22/03	28/03	1			
Determine access management/security requirements [DWK21]	5 days	22/03	28/03	1	4		4
Determine system/hardware disaster recovery requirements [DWK23]	5 days	22/03	28/03	1	1		4
Determine service desk and desktop services requirements [DWK25]	5 days	22/03	28/03	1	1	1	1
Determine IT operations requirements [DWK27]	5 days	22/03	28/03	1	1	1	1
Determine environmental and facilities requirements [DWK29]	5 days	22/03	28/03	1	1	1	1
Determine and document data requirements [DWK15]	20 days	29/03	25/04	2	10	20	46

Table continues

Table G.1 continued

Task name	Duration	Start date (dd/mm)	Finish date (dd/mm)	PO	PM	PMP	Role BA	TA	CS	PT
Determine and document organizational and FTE requirements	5 days	29/03	04/04	4	4		4	8		
Determine and document roll-out requirements and approach (complete the deployment strategy and plan) – phased, big bang etc. [DWK17]. Ensure INI11, DWK11 and DWK13 are pasted into DWK17	5 days	29/03	04/04	2	4	4	4	16		
Review detailed process design with process owner, process manager and key stakeholders for validation and approval	5 days	29/03	04/04	4	4	4		4		
Update project plan	5 days	29/03	04/04		1	1				
Obtain design phase sign-off	5 days	29/03	04/04	1	1	1				
BUILD	98 days	25/02	10/07							
Process solution build	44 days	25/02	25/04							
Finalize process workflow	44 days	25/02	25/04	1	12		1			
Draft process policy [BPS01]	44 days	25/02	25/04	1	12		1			
Draft process plan [BPS03]	44 days	25/02	25/04	3	24		8			
Draft process SOP [BPS05]	44 days	25/02	25/04	6	60		30			
Update requirement traceability matrix (RTM)	34 days	11/03	25/04	1	12		6	6		
Infrastructure build	51 days	29/03	07/06							
Procure hardware	20 days	29/03	25/04					15		

Procure software	20 days	29/03	25/04			10
Create development and test environments	10 days	29/04	10/05			55
Finalize technical solution specifications	20 days	29/04	24/05	2	8	130
Build and unit-test integrations solution	30 days	29/04	07/06			70
Build and unit-test configuration solution (menu, services, security)	30 days	29/04	07/06			120
Build and unit-test automated discovery solution	30 days	29/04	07/06			150
Build and unit-test forms/GUI solution	30 days	29/04	07/06		8	90
Build and unit-test notification solution	30 days	29/04	07/06			25
Build and unit-test technical solution	30 days	29/04	07/06		8	
Document technical solution	20 days	13/05	07/06		4	
Data solution build	36 days	26/04	14/06			
Finalize data solution specifications	30 days	26/04	06/06	2	8	70
Build data solution – interfaces etc.	30 days	26/04	06/06		4	140
Prepare data for extraction, translation and load (ETL)	25 days	13/05	14/06		4	50
Measurement build	30 days	26/04	06/06			
Finalize reporting solution specifications [BMS01]	10 days	26/04	09/05	2	24	35
Build measurement capability	10 days	26/04	09/05		4	35
Build measurement reports	20 days	10/05	06/06		4	35

Table continues

Table G.1 continued

Task name	Duration	Start date (dd/mm)	Finish date (dd/mm)	PO	PM	PMP	BA	TA	CS	PT
Training build										
Identify training groups	20 days	26/04	23/05	2	2			2		
Develop training materials [BTS01]	20 days	26/04	23/05	2	24		24	8		
Organizational build	20 days	26/04	23/05							
Build new job definitions if needed	20 days	26/04	23/05	2	4					
Build new organizational charts if needed	20 days	26/04	23/05	1	2			1		
Test plan build	43 days	29/04	26/06							
Create test plan [TPB01]	10 days	29/04	10/05	1	8		4	4		24
Create system/distribution test cases [BTP03]	20 days	16/05	12/06		24		24	24		12
Create ETL test case	20 days	16/05	12/06		4		4	45		
Create reporting test case	20 days	16/05	12/06		8		8	8		16
Create integration test case	20 days	16/05	12/06		16		16	8		24
Create user acceptance test (UAT) case	10 days	13/06	26/06		16					24
Identify and create required test data (accounts, CIs, services, work groups etc.)	30 days	16/05	26/06		8		8	16		16
Implementation plan build	10 days	27/06	10/07							
Create communication and education plan [BIP01]	5 days	27/06	03/07	2	8		4	2	24	
Develop implementation strategy and build process release [BIP03]	10 days	27/06	10/07	2	16	16	4	15	4	
Obtain build phase sign-off	5 days	03/07	09/07	2	4	4	2	2		

TEST	39 days	10/06	01/08				
Perform system testing of process solution	20 days	10/06	05/07		16	16	24
Perform system testing of infrastructure solution	20 days	10/06	05/07		8	8	20	24
Perform system testing of ETL solution	20 days	10/06	05/07		4	4	45	24
Perform system testing of reporting solution	20 days	10/06	05/07		8	8	16	16
Perform integration tests	10 days	28/06	11/07		8	8	16	16
Test training programme	10 days	28/06	11/07	2	24	24	4	4
Solicit and train users for UAT	5 days	05/07	11/07	2	8			
Perform UAT	5 days	12/07	18/07		8	4	8	
Document test results and known errors [TPB02, TPB03]	34 days	10/06	25/07		8	8	12	24
Find improvements, make improvements, and retest	5 days	26/07	01/08		8	8	8	8
Obtain test phase sign-off	5 days	26/07	01/08	2	4	4	4	
IMPLEMENT	**66 days**	**12/07**	**11/10**					
Release preparation	40 days	12/07	05/09					
Create knowledge articles [IRP01]	20 days	12/07	08/08	1	8	8	12	4
Finalize release plan	20 days	12/07	08/08	2	8	4	24	4
Finalize process policy	20 days	12/07	08/08	1	6	8	1	
Finalize process plan	20 days	12/07	08/08	3	12	4		

Table continues

Table G.1 continued

Task name	Duration	Start date (dd/mm)	Finish date (dd/mm)	PO	PM	PMP	Role BA	TA	CS	PT
Finalize process SOP	20 days	12/07	08/08	6	20		20			
Finalize training content	20 days	12/07	08/08	4	16		16	4		4
Communicate project status, content and schedule	20 days	12/07	08/08	2	8	4	8	4	8	
Schedule and deliver training	15 days	09/08	29/08	2	12		6	4		
Assign process roles to people	15 days	09/08	29/08	2	2					
Complete the 'transition requirements' section of [DWK27]	15 days	09/08	29/08	2	2	2				
Complete the transition acceptance template [IRP02] and implementation checklist [IRP03]	15 days	09/08	29/08	2	2	2	2	2		
Create and approve change order	5 days	30/08	05/09	1	4	4		4		
Release roll-out	25 days	09/09	11/10							
Publish knowledge articles	5 days	09/09	13/09		8		4	2		
Publish process policy, plan and SOP	5 days	09/09	13/09		4					
Communicate release content, WIIFM, contacts etc.	5 days	09/09	13/09	2	8	4	8		8	
Load data to production	5 days	09/09	13/09					24		
Release infrastructure solution	5 days	09/09	13/09	2	8	4	8	24	6	
Release organizational solution	5 days	09/09	13/09	2	8	4	4	4		
Release ETL solution	5 days	09/09	13/09	2	4	4	2	16		
Release reporting and measurement solution	5 days	09/09	13/09	2	8	4	4	8		
Provide early life support	20 days	16/09	11/10	2	40		40	65		

CLOSE	20 days	16/09	11/10					
Provide coaching	20 days	16/09	11/10	2	40		40	5
Monitor and review process	20 days	16/09	11/10	2	10		10	10
Document lessons learned, post-implementation review [CLS01]	20 days	16/09	11/10	2	8	8	8	8
Adjust process based on review	20 days	16/09	11/10	2	12		8	8
Approve revised process	20 days	16/09	11/10	2				
Obtain approval to close project	20 days	16/09	11/10	2	2	4		
Disband project team	20 days	16/09	11/10			1		
Close project	20 days	16/09	11/10			8		
			Total	56	364	65	293	361	26	148

187

Appendix H Communication plan template

Table H.1 is a template that can be used for documenting and recording your process communication plan. Use this document to plan and capture the communications that will need to occur throughout the process development/improvement lifecycle. Consider the following potential audiences who may need to receive communications: customers/users, project team, governance committees, IT leadership, IT staff and suppliers.

Table H.1 Communication plan

Message/goal	Audience	Frequency	Delivery method	Due date (for review)	Publication date	Content owner

Index

baselines 111
brainstorming 52–4
business cases 130–5
business functions 4
business relationship managers 97

CAP (capacity management) 82
Capability Maturity Model Integration (CMMI) 115
capacity management (CAP) 82
categorization 24–6, 40–4, 43–4, 173–4
cause identification 48–50
CFG (configuration management) 80
change management (CHM) 78–9
change managers 97
CHM (change management) 78–9
chronological analysis 54–6
CI (configuration items) 10
closure 70–3, 151, 166
CMDB (configuration management databases) 10, 41
CMMI (Capability Maturity Model Integration) 115
communication 121, 127
communication plan template 189
complementary roles 96–7
configuration items (CI) 10
configuration management (CFG) 80
configuration management databases (CMDB) 10, 41
configuration management systems 10, 41
control points 44
crime scene investigation 69
critical success factors (CSFs) 110–11, 112
customers 3, 10

data analysis 48–9
data collection 48

detection and categorization 40–4, 151, 153–6

early adopters 136
email 4
escalations 29, 30–2
executive sponsorship 125

fault tree analysis 64–6
financial management (FIN) 81–2
fire-fighting 130
fishbone diagrams 56–8
Five Whys technique 51–2
functional escalation 30–2
functional teams 5, 8–9, 86–7
functions 8–9

hierarchical escalation 32

impact 26–9
INC (incident management) 15–34, 78, 124–5
incident categorization 24–6
incident escalations 29, 30–2
incident identification 20
incident logging 20–3
incident management (INC) 15–34, 78, 124–5
incident managers 97
incident matching 16, 32–3
incident prioritization 26–32
incident records 17
incidents 10
initial diagnosis 32–4
investigation and diagnosis 44–66, 151, 158–60
Ishikawa diagrams 56–8
ISO/IEC 33001:2015 115

IT service management (ITSM)
  benefits 2–3
  definitions 9–10
  meaning of 1–4
  and problem management 86–8
  terms 9–10
  tools 125–7
IT service providers 3
IT services 4
ITSM see IT service management

job descriptions 91

Kepner-Tregoe 60–4
key performance indicators (KPIs) 111–13
KNM (knowledge management) 80–1
knowledge bases 10
knowledge management (KNM) 80–1
knowledge managers 97
known error databases 10, 48
known errors 10, 16, 32–3, 46–8
KPIs (key performance indicators) 111–13

laggards 136–7
leadership 123
logging 20–3, 42–3

major incidents 30
major problem reviews 74–5
management reporting 113–15, 128
matching 32–3, 44
measurement 109–21
metrics 111

organizational change 135–8
organizational models 101–5
outcomes 3

Pareto analysis 58–60
PDCA (Plan–Do–Check–Act) cycle 2
pitfalls 130
Plan–Do–Check–Act (PDCA) cycle 2

plans 7, 145
policies 7
policy template 139–43
prioritization 26–32, 43–4
priority changes 29
proactive problem management 11–14, 36, 41–2
problem analysts 95–6
problem categorization 24–6, 43–4, 173–4
problem definition 46
problem diagnosis 44–66
problem escalations 29, 30–2
problem identification 20
problem investigation 44–66
problem logging 20–3, 42–3
problem management
  activities 38
  business cases 130–5
  categorization 40–4
  closure 70–3, 151, 166
  definition 11–14
  detection and categorization 40–4, 151, 153–6
  goal of 35
  and incident management 17–19
  investigation and diagnosis 44–66, 151, 158–60
  and ITSM (IT service management) 86–8
  measurement 109–21
  organizing for 91–107
  plans 145
  policy template 139–43
  process 36–8, 124–5
  process adaption 98
  relationships 77–89
  resolution and recovery 66–70, 151, 162–4
  standard operating procedures template 147–67
problem managers 93–5
problem matching 32–3, 44
problem prioritization 26–32, 43–4

Index

problem records 16, 17, 38, 40–2
problem resolution 66–8
problems 10
process activities 151–67
process analysts 8
process documentation 6–7
process implementation 177
process improvement plans 120–1
process interactions 83–6
process managers 8
process maturity assessments 115–21
process owners 8, 92–3
process records 70–2
process roles 7–8
process targets 68–70
processes 5–7, 124–5

RACI matrix 98–101
reactive problem management 11, 36
release management (RLM) 17, 79
report specialists 97
reporting 113–15, 128
resolution and recovery 66–70, 151, 162–4
resolution codes 170
resource allocation 106–7
return on investment (ROI) 132–5
RLM (release management) 17, 79
ROI (return on investment) 132–5
roles 91, 125
root cause analysis 44–66
  cause identification 48–50
  data analysis 48–9
  data collection 48
  documentation 50
  problem definition 46
  techniques 51–66
  workaround identification 46–8
root cause codes 171
root causes 10, 16, 35–6

service desk managers 97
service disruption reports 72–3, 175–6
service level agreements (SLAs) 15
service level management (SLM) 77–8
service owners 97
SLAs (service level agreements) 15
SLM (service level management) 77–8
solution identification 67–8
solution implementation 68
solutions 10
standard operating procedures (SOPs) 7, 147–67
success factors 123–30, 138
supplier/vendor management (SUP) 82–3
symptom codes 169

task forces 105
technical support groups 8, 41, 86, 125
tiers 31–2, 87–8
training 128–9

unresolved problem records 71–2
urgency 26–9
users 10

VIPs 29
vision 123
vital business functions 4

workarounds 10, 16, 32–3, 46–8